Politics
for Evangelicals

To
Roger Fredrikson
and
Robert McClernon

Checking acc't

130950300

S P O T OBSERVATION REPORT | Army RO T C Wheaton College

CADET NAME:

DATE:

COURSE/SECTION:

DUTY POSITION:

RATING: Superior ☐ Above Average ☐ Below Average ☐

REMARKS:

SIGNATURE/TITLE OF RATER:

Complete this report in duplicate. Forward original through cadet command channels to Commandant of Cadets. Present duplicate copy to cadet. Each member in chain of command will initial and comment as appropriate, on back of original copy.

Paul Henry

Politics
for Evangelicals

Judson Press
Valley Forge

POLITICS FOR EVANGELICALS

Library of Congress Cataloging in Publication Data

Henry, Paul B.
  Politics for evangelicals.

  Includes bibliographical references.
  1. Christianity and politics.   I. Title.
BR115.P7H46   261.7   74-2893
ISBN 0-8170-0636-2

Printed in the U.S.A.

Contents

Introduction
by Mark O. Hatfield   7

Chapter One
Evangelicals and the Crisis
of the American Spirit   11

Chapter Two
Evangelical Social Ethics:
A Study in Moral Paralysis   27

Chapter Three
Coming Out of the Wilderness   59

Chapter Four
Strategies for Political Action   93

Notes   125

Cease to do evil and learn to do right,
pursue justice and champion the oppressed;
give the orphan his rights, plead the widow's cause.

Come now, let us argue it out,
    says the Lord.
Though your sins are scarlet,
    they may become white as snow;
    though they are dyed crimson,
    they may yet be like wool.

Isaiah 1:17-18, NEB

Introduction
by Senator Mark O. Hatfield

Jim Wallis editorialized in the January, 1974, issue of the *Post American* that evangelicals should not have been so deeply surprised about the abuses and corruption evidenced in our political system by the Watergate affair. If we had a more biblical view of the "powers," and their "fallen nature," Wallis argued, we would have had a deeper understanding of all the revelations that have shaken our political system so profoundly.

In my judgment, this point is valid. Recent biblical studies into the meaning of the "principalities and powers" referred to frequently in the New Testament have focused our awareness on the dimensions of corporate sin present in the structures of society. Certainly, the political events of recent months have provided startling pragmatic evidence for the relevance of these biblical truths. Yet, the facts of the matter are that evangelicals were among the last to recognize the scope of corruption revealed by the Watergate-related events.

To understand why Bible-believing Christians were so shocked by Watergate, we should recognize the schizophrenic attitude of many evangelicals toward politics. On the one hand, evangelicals have felt that politics is intrinsically "dirty business." The political system is "of the world," and inevitably corrupt. Christians should avoid involvement with "politics," and instead concentrate their energies on spiritual goals, according to this view. Frequently I am asked by fellow

Christians, "How can you be involved in politics and still be a good Christian?" That is the question prompted by the conviction that politics demands inevitable compromises with the evil of the world.

On the other hand, evangelicals on the whole believe in the intrinsic goodness of our nation, and the righteousness of our political structures. The pervasive influence of "civil religion" has taught us that the United States is a nation specially blessed, and given a unique virtue before God's eyes. Because of this divine hand upon us, the latent assumption is that America and its leaders can be guilty of no great sins. When our leaders tend to be politically conservative, rather than politically liberal, the tendency to trust in their goodness and wisdom is even greater, for most evangelicals believe that political conservatism is the natural counterpart of their conservative theology.

Watergate revealed the evangelical mind's internal contradictions about our nation's politics. Evangelicalism sensed that politics was almost necessarily corrupt; but it could not readily believe that a president, supported dominantly by the evangelical community, could conceivably be involved in corruption. So we witnessed the unique occurrence of some evangelicals who attempted to explain away individual accountability for actions by pointing to the environment of social sin throughout society. "There's a little bit of Watergate in each of us." This is certainly true, but it can also be a convenient way to exempt anyone from personal responsibility for wrongdoing.

Evangelicals have been skeptical about the virtue of politics, but convinced about the virtue of the nation. This inner division has caused many to shun meaningful political involvement and to ignore biblical teaching about the judgment of God on corporate, national sin.

In surveying the present attitudes and sensitivities within the evangelical church, however, it is clearly evident that fundamental changes are in process. Unmistakably, there is a growing awareness of the social and political dimensions of faith that are an inherent part of the whole gospel. Publications, books, conferences, and various movements all give witness to the reawakening of political awareness among evangelicals. With this has come the growing recognition that we stand corporately under God's judgment, as a people, rather than being automatically blessed in all our nation's undertakings.

Out of the contemporary political turmoil, we can rediscover that faith in Jesus Christ makes us witnesses to a new order. Because of Christ, we have the knowledge of a whole new creation; we know that our political, economic, and social structures can be continually remade to reflect God's justice, just as our individual lives are transformed to show forth the likeness of Christ.

Politics for Evangelicals is one more sign of these new, emerging currents of thoughts occurring within evangelical circles, and is indicative that the old stereotypes about politics and evangelicals are no longer credible. Paul Henry demonstrates with rich historical and theological insight why the evangelical church in America withdrew itself from the political realm during this century. He then offers concrete suggestions for those who are persuaded that this withdrawal from political involvement must be reversed.

The author is uniquely suited to write on these matters, for his own life has reflected the urge to express an evangelical faith through relevant political involvement. Paul Henry has experience in the Congress, when he served with Congressman John Anderson; he has remained actively involved in Michigan politics, while teaching political science at Calvin College. In this book, Paul Henry's academic training, political experiences, and spiritual commitment merge together. His thoughts are a testimony to the experiences of his life.

As fellow signers of the Declaration of Evangelical Social Concern, the author and I share a common commitment to act forth the impact of Christ's life on the political and social conditions of our own time. **Politics for**

Evangelicals is an expression, by Paul Henry, of this commitment, and should be edifying to many who are struggling in a new way with the meaning of their faith for their lives in this age.

If evangelicals are to avoid being surprised and shocked by political happenings in the future, and instead speak with a truly prophetic voice to our nation, then we must reconstruct a truly biblical view of our relationship to political power and our responsibility for social sin. The political crisis which has afflicted the nation can be the catalyst for the evangelical community to establish a vibrant and whole witness to a society that stands in such desperate spiritual need.

Chapter One

Evangelicals and the Crisis of the American Spirit

January 20, 1961. By Washington standards, it was a blustery cold day. The young, forty-three-year-old president-elect doffed his topcoat to repeat the brief, thirty-five-word oath of office: "I, John Fitzgerald Kennedy, do solemnly swear that I will faithfully execute the Office of President of the United States, and will to the best of my ability, preserve, protect and defend the Constitution of the United States."

Thus began the administration of a new president who had promised to "get America moving again." He was the youngest president in the history of the nation. He was the first Roman Catholic ever elected to that office. Appropriately, he stated in his inaugural address: "The torch of freedom has passed to a new generation."

Looking back, it is hard to imagine—let alone remember—the hope, the idealism, the vigor, and the youthful innocence that the Kennedy administration injected into American politics. Thousands of young people volunteered their

11

talents to the Peace Corps to evangelize the world for the American way of life. Special-force "Green Berets" fought in the jungles of Indochina to show that America would bear any cost to defend the cause of freedom. Over one hundred thousand civil-rights marchers trekked to Washington singing confidently: "Black and white together, we shall overcome someday."

November 22, 1963. A gunshot fired in Dallas, Texas, was heard around the world. The president was dead.

In retrospect, we are now able to see that the shot which felled the president represented more than the death of a national leader by the isolated act of a madman. For while Lyndon Johnson struggled mightily to wear the mantle of his predecessor and restore order, the fates of history turned on him as well. The United States, like Humpty-Dumpty, seemed to have fallen into many pieces. And nobody, it seemed, could "bring us together" again.

Young people who had just a few years earlier enthusiastically volunteered for Peace Corps service were marching to Washington to urinate on the walls of government buildings. The sweet rhetoric surrounding our military involvement in Indochina degenerated into bitter vitriol over a war for which nobody would take responsibility. Martin Luther King, Jr., was assassinated, and Stokely Carmichael and George Wallace struggled to fill the vacuum created by his passing.

The people long for a new "greening of America." But each day it seems farther away. Lyndon Johnson, who in 1964 was elected president by one of the greatest electoral margins in history, was forced to deny himself even the attempt at a second term. Of those who sought to succeed him, one was assassinated. The second term which was denied Johnson was granted to Richard Nixon, who in 1972 won a second term as president by an electoral victory which almost matched that of Lyndon Johnson in 1964. And yet within only a year of his second term, his administration was rocked by some of the greatest scandals in American history. The vice-president resigned rather than face impeachment by the Congress. The president himself governed under the threat of impeachment, his credibility called into question by the Watergate activities, the secret bombing of Cambodia, and the financing of his San Clemente estate.

What has gone wrong with America? The sweet innocence, undaunted hope, and unlimited energy of its youth seem suddenly to have been lost. Its people are distressed and disillusioned. Signs of senility—confusion, aimlessness, and exhaustion— are showing themselves increasingly in American life.

The apparent senescence of America has come to us as a great surprise, just as Woodrow Wilson had predicted when he wrote: "America is now sauntering through her resources and through the mazes of her politics with easy nonchalance; but presently there will come a time when she will be surprised to find herself grown old—a country crowded, strained, perplexed. . . ."[1] That time has come. We are not ready for it. And we wonder whether the passing of the old will make way for the new, or whether the passing of the old means death itself.

As we approach the bicentennial of the nation in 1976, an increasing number of Americans are wondering whether there will be anything left to celebrate. We are a divided people—and we know that a nation divided against itself cannot stand. Black and white, rich and poor, young and old, hawk and dove, hard hats and pointy-headed intellectuals—nothing, it seems, can bring us together again.

Technology, once viewed as a liberator, has established new forms of enslavement. Our work, values, and tastes are often dictated by corporate decisions, technological innovations, and economies of scale. Bureaucracy has so depersonalized us that we watch passively from apartment windows while women are raped in the street. The violence of war itself has become so computerized that we no longer feel anything upon learning of the latest kill-ratio results of "protective reaction strikes" against the enemy.

Our environment is rotting. Mothers' milk sometimes contains such high levels of environmental pollution that it could not be legally sold in a supermarket had it come from a cow. The average New York City resident inhales pollutants equivalent to smoking almost two packs of cigarettes a day. Life has become so bothersome for many that they seek escape with alcohol, drugs, or mystical religions.

No longer do just the extremists on the left or right voice these frustrations. It's the middle Americans—the silent majority—who can no longer remain silent. It's the voters who voted for Eugene McCarthy in the 1968 New Hampshire presidential primary—and then turned around to vote for George Wallace in the general election. It's the voters who in 1972 couldn't choose between Wallace and McGovern in the Democratic primaries.

Confidence in the institutions of our national government has dropped drastically in the past few years. In 1971, the Harris Poll reported that only 23 percent of the American public held a "great deal" of confidence in the executive branches of the federal government, and only 19 percent held a "great deal" of confidence in the Congress. In 1973, the Gallup Poll found that only 26 percent of the American public felt satisfied with the way in which the nation was being governed.[2]

In the last several elections, ticket splitting has reached an all-time high. Increasingly, Americans are refusing to identify themselves with either of the existing political parties. In a few years, it is expected that independents will outnumber either Republicans or Democrats. (They already outnumber Republicans.) Our nation is facing unprecedented problems—and "politics as usual" isn't going to solve them. The political system needs new blood before it can find new life.

The government is not the only social institution facing an acute crisis. The institutional church is also in turmoil. In 1957, 69 percent of the adult population expressed the opinion that the church was increasing its influence in American life. By 1970, that figure had more than reversed itself so that 75 percent expressed the belief that the church was losing influence in American life.[3] Is it any wonder, then, that church attendance has been dropping regularly for the last fifteen years? Is it any wonder that church membership growth is not keeping up with the population growth in the nation?

Our church leaders—seeking desperately to find new relevance to the modern world—have tried almost everything. On the one hand are those church councils which seem unable to express confidence in the historic creeds of the church; instead, they substitute political action for religious faith, revolution for regeneration, pressure politics for prayer. On the other hand are those church councils which are so concerned over the dogmatic heresy of the former that they spend their time abstracting doctrines intellectually with little if any regard for the question of relevance. One half of the church is irrelevant because it offers nothing which can't be found outside the walls of the church. The other half of the church is irrelevant because what goes on inside the walls of the church bears no relation to what goes on outside the walls of the church.

Few would doubt the assertion that the United States today is in the midst of a social upheaval. As H. L. Nieburg suggests:

> Both the sacred and profane of our mental universe are destroyed; our obscenities have been rendered pallid by overuse; the mysteries of sex have been stripped away; the demands of national security no longer provide goals for organized activity;

production and consumption as social imperatives are inverted by an ethos that apparently demands neither work nor discipline. Productivity is to be looted for its high-performance cars, high-fidelity audio, and highs of drugs and sensuality. Looting and vandalism are the order of the day, not only in public parks and school bathrooms, but everywhere that old values and institutions are found to be loose and undefended. This is the age that made the journey to the moon and found it dull and pointless. The age whose counter-culture soon became an over-the-counter-culture. The age whose revolutionary youth descended to "ripping off" cherry trees and park benches in Washington, D.C.[4]

Where was the church during this period of upheaval? More particularly, what will it do in response to the events of the last ten years? Can the church take hold of the present crisis of confidence pervading American culture and politics and provide the much needed leadership toward social renewal?

It is the thesis of this brief essay that the church can and must respond to the present malaise of the American spirit. The Good News of Jesus Christ was meant for all men for all times. And it extends to every dimension of the human predicament. But if the church is going to respond to the despair, alienation, and frustration so evident in contemporary America, it must begin by putting its own house in order.

The church must begin by transcending the polarities which presently divide those who tend to reduce the gospel to a political message on the one hand, and those who tend to reduce the gospel to spiritual abstractions on the other hand. To those who see in the gospel of Jesus Christ nothing more than a message of social and political liberation, we must proclaim the limits of politics. And to those who see in the gospel of Jesus Christ nothing more than purely spiritual escape from social and political captivity, we must proclaim the legitimacy of politics. While the gospel must never be viewed as simply political, neither must it be reduced to a form of gnosticism which fails to recognize that the message of the gospel is among other things political. (Gnosticism was one of the earliest heresies the church had to counter, and it has also proved to be one of the most enduring. Gnosticism tends to identify the struggle between good and evil as the struggle between "spirit" and "matter." Hence, gnostics have never been able to accept fully the Christian understanding of "God made flesh" and the implications of a salvation which speaks to the entire spectrum of human life.)

The humanism of modern liberalism and the gnosticism of modern neoorthodoxy and fundamentalism are both partly responsible for the present crisis in the church and society. For while the former has elevated politics as the new means of grace, the latter has so reduced the efficacy of grace that it no longer reaches down to the political needs of modern man. So long as we expend our energies pointing to the failures and inconsistencies of one party in this contest while remaining oblivious to the failures and inconsistencies of the other, we are simply engaging in an ecclesiastical tug-of-war between two teams of pious hypocrites. Meanwhile, life around us degenerates into hell on earth. Both sides are subject to the judgment of God. And both sides must repent of the institutional pride and jealousy which has hardened their hearts against the full counsel of God as taught in the Scriptures.

Let both sides in this contest begin by acknowledging the limits of politics. The crisis of the present is in part the result of our belief that politics can save us. This belief is based on the assumption that man is individually righteous and that only social systems render him corrupt. Given the proper social system, the true essence of man will ultimately shine forth. Is it any wonder, then, that the radical left blames the *system* for the social and economic and political inequalities and inequities of the present age? For if man is good, then the system must be bad.

But if this is the case, what accounts for the pervasiveness of the present crisis of confidence in American institutions? The United States, for all of its faults, has achieved a relatively just social system—and yet the intensity of the political and social despair is increasing. Does the reason lie in the fact that we are discovering that the god of politics is not the God of salvation? Belatedly, increasing numbers of political observers have been answering this question in the affirmative.

Daniel P. Moynihan, adviser to Presidents Johnson and Nixon, has declared:

> The principal issues of the moment are not political. They are seen as such: That is the essential clue to their nature. But the crisis of the time is not political, it is in essence religious. It is a religious crisis of large numbers of intensely moral, even Godly, people who no longer hope for God. Hence, the quest for divinity assumes a secular form, but with an intensity of conviction that is genuinely new to our politics.[5]

Henry A. Kissinger, President Nixon's foreign-policy adviser and secretary of state, continues on this theme when he states:

> The modern bureaucratic state, for all its panoply of strength, often finds itself shaken to its foundations by seemingly trivial causes. Its brittleness and the world-wide revolution of youth—especially in advanced countries and among the relatively affluent—suggest a spiritual void, an almost metaphysical boredom with a political environment that increasingly emphasizes bureaucratic challenges and is dedicated to no deeper purpose than material comfort.[6]

In the words of Senator Mark O. Hatfield, "Our nation's foremost need is the recovery of a relevant moral conscience. Ultimately, that can only be done through individuals, not by the state."[7] And voicing convictions similar to those of Hatfield, Senator Harold E. Hughes announced that when his term in the Senate expired, he would retire from politics so that he could devote all of his time to Christian evangelism.

Government and politics have not only become substitutes for God in American culture, but we demand more of them than we demanded of God when we believed in him. Samuel Lubell, a noted scholar of American politics, has written:

> The Bible and sermons assured us that God, as the Over-all Manager, was all-wise, all-powerful and all-knowing, even to being able to account for every swallow's whereabouts. Still, He was not expected to perform His miracles until the afterworld. Today we demand that government deliver on sight.[8]

The social gospel, based on the assumption of man's innate goodness and dedicated to the creation of a political society where men will attain perfect freedom, ultimately leads to the despair of totalitarianism. For if man is good, the fact that goodness does not prevail can only be explained by reasoning that the power necessary to liberate man from his present bondage has been frustrated. The solution is obvious: give complete, unlimited, and total power to those who share the vision of the perfect society.

The blame for the present crisis in American politics rests, however, not only on the shoulders of those who have misplaced faith in God for faith in politics, but also on those who in the name of God have denied the full legitimacy of politics. In responding to the misplaced faith of liberal humanism, theological conservatives have tended to respond to the demands of politics in one of two ways. At worst, they have shunned politics as a dirty, worldly, and humanistic endeavor alien to the concerns of the gospel. At best, they have regarded politics as a legitimate enterprise only when placing it at a level of secondary importance to the "church's primary task of preaching the gospel." What both groups of conservatives have failed to see is that the gospel itself is, among other things, a gospel of political redemption. Conservatives have so often spiritualized the gospel as to be guilty of practicing a modern form of gnosticism—surely a heresy no worse than the humanism of the theological liberals. Theological conservatives must recognize that political concerns are not simply incidental to the message of the gospel, but integral to the very meaning of the gospel itself.

Conservatives have virtually immunized

themselves from recognizing the political dimensions of the gospel. They are almost blind to the fact that the birth, life, and death of the Messiah were interpreted among his contemporaries in political terms. Conservatives have emphasized the priestly function of the incarnation at the expense of the prophetic and kingly functions which were all to be united in the Messiah.

The political character of the gospel has its roots in the prophetic tradition of the Old Testament—a tradition which continually resurfaces throughout the entire New Testament. As early as the angel Gabriel's annunciation to the Virgin Mary, political overtones are present in the gospel. ". . . You shall conceive and bear a son . . . and he will be king over Israel for ever; his reign shall never end" (Luke 1:31, 33). Mary's response in the celebrated Magnificat clearly anticipates a connection between this new king and political and social justice:

> "the arrogant of heart and mind he has put to rout,
> he has brought down monarchs from their thrones,
>   but the humble have been lifted high.
> The hungry he has satisfied with good things,
>   the rich sent empty away."
>
> Luke 1:51-53

Zechariah, father of John the Baptist, acknowledged that this was the time in which the God of Israel had "raised up a deliverer of victorious power" who would "deliver us from our enemies, out of the hands of all who hate us . . ." (Luke 1:69; 71). In God's good mercy and due time,

> ". . . in the tender compassion of our God
>   the morning sun from heaven will rise upon us,

to shine on those who live in darkness, under the cloud of death,
and to guide our feet into the way of peace."

Luke 1:78-79

The circumstances surrounding Christ's birth were so politically explosive that King Herod consulted his court astrologists, lawyers, and priests to try to put together the meaning of the event. Fearful that the newly born "King of the Jews" would rival his own claim to power, he gave the fateful order that in the area of Bethlehem all male children under two years of age were to be slain.

As the young Christ child matured and "advanced in wisdom and in favour with God and men," John the Baptist proclaimed not only "baptism in token of repentance for the forgiveness of sins," but also the coming of the kingdom of God as anticipated by the prophet Isaiah:

> "Every ravine shall be filled in,
> and every mountain and hill levelled;
> the corners shall be straightened,
> and the rugged ways made smooth;
> and all mankind shall see God's deliverance."

Luke 3:5-6

John the Baptist's message was directly connected with pleas for social justice: ". . . prove your repentance by the fruit it bears. The man with two shirts must share with him who has none, and anyone who has food must do the same." To the tax collectors and soldiers, John proclaimed: "Exact no more than the assessment. No bullying; no blackmail; make do with your pay!" (See Luke 3:8-14.)

Christ himself proclaimed the social implications of the new kingdom as foretold by Isaiah:

"The spirit of the Lord is upon me because he has
    anointed me;
he has sent me to announce good news to the poor,
to proclaim release for prisoners and recovery of sight
    for the blind;
to let the broken victims go free,
to proclaim the year of the Lord's favour."

Luke 4:18-19

While liberal theologians have sometimes failed to
recognize that the gospel teaches repentance and
remission of sins, evangelical theologians have just
as often failed to recognize the ethical demands of the
gospel. "Alas for you Pharisees! You pay tithes of
mint and rue and every garden-herb, but have no care
for justice and the love of God. It is these you should
have practised, without neglecting the others" (Luke
11:42).

Evangelicals have so spiritualized the demands of
the kingdom of God upon temporal life that the
Sermon on the Mount is viewed not as a list of moral
imperatives for Christian action, but as a set of "be-
attitudes" present in the heart of the properly pious
believer. James suggested the following test for
religious orthodoxy, however: "The kind of religion
which is without stain or fault in the sight of God
our Father is this: to go to the help of orphans and
widows in their distress and keep oneself untar-
nished by the world" (James 1:27). Yet, the
evangelical test for orthodoxy is more than likely
mastery of speculations concerning the "rapture"
and God's future kingdom rather than any practical
accomplishments in the building of God's present
kingdom.

While they are correct in recognizing that the

kingdom of God is not a kingdom of the world, evangelicals have nonetheless failed to recognize that the two realms are closely connected; for our citizenship in the kingdom of God entails moral obligations for our citizenship in the kingdoms of men. Peter captures the ethical implications of being God's children in this world when he states:

> Since the whole universe is to break up in this way, think what sort of people you ought to be, what devout and dedicated lives you should live! Look eagerly for the coming of the Day of God and *work to hasten it on;* that day will set the heavens ablaze until they fall apart, and will melt the elements in flames. But we have his promise, and look forward to new heavens and a new earth, *the home of justice* (2 Peter 3:11-13, emphasis mine).

The existence of two camps of Christians, each of which emphasizes one-half of the gospel message at the expense of the other, is becoming intolerable to increasing numbers of thoughtful individuals who believe that God demands faithfulness in both creed and deed. And yet in the institutional life of the church, one is too often forced to choose between either dogmatic orthodoxy or ethical orthodoxy.

There are signs—particularly in the evangelical community—that this "either/or" dichotomy of Christian commitment is being overcome. And it is within this context of evangelical self-examination and renewal that this little volume has been written.

Americans are increasingly convinced that our nation is undergoing a crisis of the spirit. Its soul is being tested. As one commentator puts it:

> As a nation, we have lost faith. We have become self-conscious and self-critical as a whole people. No longer the exclusive province of the intellectual, the moral decrepitude of the nation is taken for granted even by the plastic middle Americans. . . .

Chapter Two

Evangelical Social Ethics:
A Study in Moral Paralysis

Knowledgeable observers—even those committed to an evangelical theology—generally concede that twentieth-century evangelicalism has failed to develop a mature social ethic or political strategy. Indeed, the basic apologetic tenor of the evangelical movement is still focused essentially on relating Christian faith to the natural sciences, despite the fact that increasing numbers of individuals find greater apologetic difficulty in relating Christian faith to the concerns of the social sciences. On a day-to-day basis, the Christian must relate his faith more frequently and more thoughtfully to the theories of social revolution than those of natural evolution. When is the last time somebody told you he turned against the church because he was unable to reconcile the Genesis creation accounts with the demands of modern science? On the other hand, have you not encountered individuals who left the church because they saw the church as an impediment to achieving social justice?

Indeed, many historians of science argue that Christian concepts of nature actually provided the intellectual foundations for the development of modern science. On the other hand, there is no shortage of social historians today who would share the dictum of Karl Marx that religious faith is an opiate which diffuses the struggle for social justice by transferring attention from man's present physical plight to his future spiritual bliss.

One would be hard put to provoke an argument in an evangelical church today as to whether or not Christian faith could be made compatible to the demands of modern science. But the relation between Christian faith and the social order is so potentially explosive that our pulpits abstain from giving us instruction where it is most needed. The concept of separation of church and state means, for much of the evangelical community, a separation of religion and politics.

What accounts for the silence of the evangelical community in the social arena? Why the lack of serious attention to social problems by the established leadership of evangelicalism? The silence of the evangelical church today stands against its own tradition of social pronouncement and social activism. Evangelicals have wandered far away from the likes of the pulpiteer Jonathan Boucher (1738–1804), who preached with two loaded pistols on the pulpit to defend himself against his angered congregation! In the mid-nineteenth century, the famous evangelical pulpit of Park Street Church was one of the few in the Boston area made available to

the crusading abolitionist William Lloyd Garrison.
Jonathan Blanchard, the first president of Wheaton
College (Illinois), was not only an active
abolitionist, but he also protested against commer-
cial activities on the Lord's Day by leading sit-down
demonstrations on the railroad tracks running
through the community. What has caused the
evangelical community of twentieth-century
America to abandon its social activism and its
commitment toward creating a just and righteous
society? To answer this question, we must first look
at some of the factors which have informed, shaped,
and limited the development of a mature social ethic
in contemporary evangelicalism.

Individualism

American political culture is based upon a highly
individualistic concept of man and society.
Evangelicals have generally tended to be part of that
individualistic culture rather than to stand against
it—even though in some respects it violates biblical
concepts pertaining to the social nature of man and
the corporate moral responsibilities of societies.

The individualism in American political life has
its origins in several sources. But without doubt the
most important of these is that general body of
liberal political theory influenced by John Locke
(1632–1704). Locke's political writings were offered
as a defense of the English Revolution of 1688, and
the American colonists were quick to give Locke a
quick baptism in order to use his arguments on
behalf of their own revolution of 1776.

So great has been the impact of Lockean political thought upon American political culture that one scholar remarks that all Americans are born as Lockean liberals.[1] The principles of Locke are part of the American birthright, and to repudiate them is, in part, to repudiate America itself.

Locke argued that all mankind is born into a state of nature which operates under laws which can be made self-evident to the inquiring mind. These laws, both physical and moral, establish a natural harmony in the universe and provide a framework of moral responsibility to which all men are obligated.

However, it was very obvious to Locke in the seventeenth century—a period of great political unrest in his own country—that the supposed euphony of society had degenerated into cacophony. This occurred, argued Locke, because society had reached a level of complexity in which the laws pertaining to it had become equally complex. Hence, there was a need for specialists to find, interpret, and enforce the laws of nature and to pass human laws of convenience which would direct the society into its natural state of harmony. Therefore, individuals create government on the basis of a social contract to handle this difficult task. Since government is created to enunciate, refine, and enforce these natural laws, it has authority only insofar as its actions are in keeping with the natural law. When government violates the natural law, it violates the contract by which it is established and revolution against it is justified.

There are several important implications of

Locke's theory which, when pointed out, can be recognized as very much a part of the American political consciousness. _First_ is the concept that society and government are created by the individuals of whom they are composed. Government and society exist to serve the individual, not vice versa. _Second,_ the function of government is really quite limited—to clarify, enunciate, and enforce the laws of nature. Once this is accomplished, there is a sort of natural harmony which will govern relations between men. Government does not exist to meddle with the laws of nature or to interfere with the natural balance within nature. _Third,_ since government is created by the people for this specific task, should it ever violate or exceed the task assigned to it, the people have the right to abolish it. The overall task of government is to maximize individual freedoms by perfecting the laws upon which individual freedom rests. In this sense, government may be said to provide for the general welfare of all.

As the scientific revolution—and the social and technological revolutions spurred by it—began to affect society, the goal of a society in which the benefit of all was achieved by maximizing individual freedom in the Lockean sense became increasingly illusory. Technology began to place disproportionate power in the hands of its masters at the expense of the masses. Further, no individual could ever achieve autonomous freedom in a technological society which bred increasing degrees of specialization and interdependence.

Hence, in the twentieth century, many individuals

challenged the "classical liberalism" of Locke with a "modern liberalism" which suggested that government must assume a more active role in regulating the lives of individuals. The cause of maximizing personal freedoms for all people could be better achieved if, in some instances, we placed limited restraints on the freedoms of others. Hence, the distinction between classical liberalism and modern liberalism has been at the heart of the distinction between "conservatism" and "liberalism" in the lexicon of contemporary American politics.

But for all their apparent differences, even modern liberals share the fundamental assumptions of Locke that (1) government is a product of the collective consent of individuals, (2) the purpose of government is to maximize the total amount of individual freedom, and (3) a government which violates its trust is properly the object of revolution. The real differences between conservatives and liberals in the American tradition are those of means, not of ends or of fundamental suppositions about the origins, purposes, and authority of government.

If we look at the Lockean credo from a biblical perspective, however, we find several points of conflict. The *first* regards the nature of man. Locke sees man as essentially autonomous. The purpose of government is, therefore, to perfect and protect his autonomy. The Bible, on the other hand, portrays a picture of man as a social being. God created man and woman so that neither would be alone. (See Genesis 2:18-25.) The nature of the church is pictured as one of extreme interdependence between the parts, each of which has a gift which contributes to the others. (See 1 Corinthians 12.) We are pictured in the Bible as being responsible not only for our own well-being, but also for the well-being of our brother.

What Locke has done is to elevate the concept of man's *selfishness* as a principle for social organization. Society exists only for the collective wills of the selves of which it is composed. The Lockean model of the autonomous man differs quite drastically from the Christian model of the "man for others."

Second, Locke's concept of the origin of government must also be called into question. Romans 13 rather clearly teaches that government is more than a human convenience. It is divinely ordained and serves divine purposes as well as being humanly instituted and serving human purposes. It is questionable as to whether Locke's argument regarding the "social contract" origin of government was meant to be taken as anything more than an allegorical analogy. Nonetheless, it contrasts sharply with the biblical model of government as an instrument established in the will of God—that rulers on earth are in the last analysis but vice-regents of God's own ordering of the universe.

Third, one must question the purpose of government as it has been defined by the Lockean tradition. For Locke, government exists to prescribe and enforce the natural law for the sake of maximizing individual freedom. Insofar as Locke saw individual freedom as operating under the restraints of "natural law," it may be said that Locke recognized that

freedom cannot be separated from moral responsibility and self-restraint. However, the tradition
descending from Locke has tended to emphasize
individual freedom as opposed to defining the
natural law (moral responsibility and restraints)
under which freedom is said to operate. The logical
outcome of Lockean liberalism in this sense leads to
anarchy, of which Marxism is but a variant. (Marx
simply wished to get back to the pure state of nature
in which the state would no longer be necessary to
maintain order.)

Christ, too, was concerned with human freedom.
But rather than viewing freedom descriptively as the
simple absence of restraint, as the Lockean tradition
tends to do, he defined freedom substantively as a life
lived in accordance with the will of God. ". . . You
shall know the truth, and the truth will set you free.
. . . Everyone who commits sin is a slave. . . . If then
the Son sets you free, you will indeed be free" (John
8:32-36).

Fourth, one must question the almost simplistic
notion of revolution handed down to us from the
Lockean tradition. Most middle Americans are now
so comfortable with the status quo that the thought
of there being any inherent right of revolution for
those who don't share as generously in the goods of
society is most disquieting. They would like to forget
that Thomas Jefferson postulated that in a true
republic a revolution would occur roughly every
twenty-five years, and that even good old Abe
Lincoln insisted that Americans had the
"revolutionary right to dismember or overthrow"

their government when they "grow weary of the existing government."

Such a teaching not only violates the tradition of the greater part of classical and medieval political theory, but also flies in the face of the apparent biblical injunctions and the traditional teachings of the church in support of obedience to political authority.

These remarks are not to be taken as a flat-out repudiation of the liberal tradition's high regard for consensual politics or individual rights and human freedom. For the individualist bent of American politics has made tremendous contributions toward a truly humane social order. The point is that one must not yield to the tradition uncritically.

For there have also been great costs associated with these gains. We have in many respects been blinded to the social dimensions of human existence. And while the Lockean tradition has heightened our sensitivity and capacity to appreciate the *personal* dimension of human responsibility and fulfillment, it has lowered our sensitivity and capacity to appreciate the *social* dimension of human responsibility and fulfillment.

We fail to see that society is more than a collection of individual wills contracting together at a point in time. Societies are also the products of the past and have obligations toward the future. And they carry moral responsibility for not only the present, but for the past and the future as well.

We fail to see that God judges not only individuals and individual actions, but also societies and social actions. And although our lives have become increasingly interdependent and intertwined with the lives of others, we continue to be guided by an ethic which is unable to address itself to the corporate dimensions of sin, righteousness, and human responsibility.

We conveniently forget that the Old Testament prophets called down God's judgment upon entire nations for their rebellion against God's ordinances—obviously, holding the entire societies collectively responsible before God. For example, God's punishment of Sodom and Gomorrah was placed upon the entire communities—not just the unrighteous individuals within them. God held the "righteous" individuals in those societies responsible for the iniquity which abounded in their communities. And we fail to recognize that the New Testament paradigm for God's people is the new "city" of God established amidst cities of men. Hence, we address the deity as *"Our* Father which art in heaven. . . ." And John's Revelation judges the seven churches of Asia as collective entities, not simply in terms of the individuals of which they are composed.

We must come to see that nations—just as individuals—may be said to have a spiritual life that leads either to felicity or damnation. The status of a nation's spiritual health projects a moral climate which fundamentally affects the public policies a nation pursues. In other words, nations may be said, in an allegorical sense, to possess a soul. And just as the outward life of an individual reflects the spiritual resources and commitments of his soul, so, too, the outward life of a state reflects the spiritual resources and commitments of its soul.

The individualist biases of American political culture encourage us to see the state and society as nothing more than the sum product of their components, as opposed to recognizing that in some important respects state and society have a life and impact of their own which in turn affect the character of the component parts. There is a two-way, reciprocal relationship between the group and the individual.

Nonetheless, evangelical ethics by and large continue to see social betterment as a simple, almost automatic, by-product of personal evangelism; and it sees in personal evangelism the only genuine route to social reform. Thus, Billy Graham captures the spirit of the evangelical approach to social problems by insisting that really there are no social problems—only composites of individual problems. Just as John Locke might say that there really is no such thing as a society or a state—just composites of individuals choosing to call themselves that—so Billy Graham can write:

> The international problems are only reflections of individual problems. Sin is sin, be it personal or social, and the word "repent" is inseparably bound up with "evangelism." Social sins, after all, are merely a large-scale projection of individual sins and need to be repented of by the offending segment of society.[2]

Negative View of the State

Evangelicals have rather uncritically accepted yet another characteristic of American political culture.

Rather than viewing government positively as a gift from God (as we are enjoined to do in Romans 13), evangelicals have generally viewed government indifferently, as a necessary evil. They have tended to subscribe to a negative view of the state which is fearful of any and all government power. Rather than seeing in government one of the great achievements of mankind which distinguishes human society from brute animal existence, evangelicals have seen government itself as a leviathan seeking to devour our freedoms. Rather than regarding government as providing opportunities for Christian leadership in society, evangelicals share in the popular disdain of politicians and officeholders as a breed of megalomaniacs.

What accounts for such suspicion and distrust of government? Why do we so simplistically accept such statements as "That government which governs best, governs least"? For surely the logical extension of this would be a commitment to anarchy. If the government which governs least is best, then the best government would be that which governs not at all!

There are two basic sources of this negative assessment of state power within the American evangelical community. The first is rooted in the American historical experience. The second is rooted in a rather uncritical acceptance of St. Augustine's teachings regarding the state.

The American historical experience fostered a negative view of the state insofar as self-conscious Americanism has its origins to a large extent in the struggle for independence *against* another government. The independence struggle saw the dangers inherent in government power which was distant from the people. Further, since the struggle for independence was personified into a struggle against the British monarchy, the Americans came to distrust executive power in particular. Thus, the first attempt at American union under the Articles of Confederation established a central government with no executive head, and with powers so limited as to make the government of the confederation inoperative. When, under the Constitution, the American government was reconstituted to give the central government more power, the Congress was still maintained as the "first branch" of government. The role of Congress was viewed, among other things, as that of checking the power of the executive. The prevailing American view was—and in some respects still is—that freedom is won against the excesses of government. The more one succeeds in limiting government, the more one succeeds in protecting his freedom.

Obviously there is some merit to this position—but only within certain limits. A strong case may be made that governments have historically interfered with what we presently regard as the private rights of individuals. In this sense, we can view many of the present social and political liberties of our society as having been the product of a strongly *limited* government.

But one must caution against the danger of absolutizing freedom at the expense of order. And one must also guard against insisting that any extension of government activity is *ipso facto* harmful to the cause of freedom. A government which posts speed limits for automotive traffic is limiting our freedom to travel at any speed whenever we desire—but the net impact is to provide a context of order in which the right to travel and other related rights are all made more secure. A government which regulates the sale of stocks and bonds may be placing limits on the freedom of the entrepreneur pushing various securities—but it makes more secure the property of the potential investor. What is important in assessing governmental action from a libertarian point of view is not simply the extension of government intrusion into our lives, but the net impact of government policies on our freedoms. From this point of view, one can see that freedoms are won not only *against* government, but also *through* government.

This is, of course, a very sensitive issue in the current world struggle between those countries committed to open societies sustained by limited governments and those countries committed to closed societies sustained by totalitarian governments. We have grown accustomed to referring to the latter as police states because the governments of these societies seek to police every aspect of human behavior. However, we should be reminded that limited governments often behave like police states, although in a different sense. It was a revolutionary Marxist, Ferdinand Lassalle, who first coined the term "police state" when he condemned the weaknesses of a strictly limited government as follows:

> This is a policeman's idea, gentlemen, a policeman's idea for this reason, because it represents to itself the State from a point of view of a policeman, whose whole function consists in preventing robbery and burglary.[3]

Too often, evangelicals have blindly accepted arguments for limiting government action to combat social evil in the mistaken belief that expanded governmental intervention is necessarily a greater evil than that to which it is directed. And through this, the well-intentioned convictions of evangelicals have been exploited by those who benefit from the government's inability to attack social evil and injustice. Thus, the *New York Times* has asserted that the famed evangelist Billy Sunday was subsidized by the business community "as a police measure—as a means of keeping the lower classes quiet."[4]

Evangelicals have been so overly concerned about the positive uses of government power that they have simplistically equated social welfare measures with outright socialism, and socialism with outright communism. Richard Pierard summarizes this attitude as follows:

> Schemes such as urban renewal, public housing, Medicare, and Social Security are part of a gigantic conspiracy to undermine the free institutions of the United States. . . . Christians should resist all "socialist tendencies." This viewpoint has been expressed with varying degrees of intensity by evangelical leaders. . . . Harold John Ockenga was quoted in the N.A.E. organ as saying that socialist schemes "soften society for Marxism," while Albert J. Lindsey told an N.A.E. convention in Chicago that socialism is "nothing more than a prep school for communism."[5]

But as we have already indicated, the evangelical's negative view of the state is rooted not only in the American experience, but also in the impact of Augustinian thought upon Christian social ethics. Indeed, the impact of St. Augustine's thought has been so pervasive that one observer has commented: "Especially in the area of social philosophy Augustine's influence is determinative for the West."[6]

What was Augustine's teaching about the state? And why has it played such an important role in the subsequent social teachings of the church? In order to answer these questions, we must first of all briefly deal with the dilemma of the early Christian community in developing an appropriate attitude toward the state. The term "dilemma" is appropriate—for we find that the early church had little by way of systematic thought on the nature of politics and political society, and it was to this void that St. Augustine sought to address himself.

We must remember that despite the political and social implications of Christ's messiahship, he nonetheless avoided any direct endorsement or entanglement with the political factions of his time. Although God in Christ was made flesh and the kingdom of God was proclaimed to be at hand, the mission of Christ and the nature of his kingdom transcended the limitations of the politics of his time.

During his ministry, Christ passed prophetic judgment on each of the major political groupings of his day. Although his triumphal entry into

Jerusalem for the Passover festival seemingly complimented the ambitions of the Zealots, who sought a revolutionary overthrow of the Roman occupation, his repudiation of Peter's use of the sword against a Roman soldier clearly dissociated him from zealotry. Although his retreat into the wilderness and his baptism by John the Baptist suggest ties to the Essenes (a group practicing ascetic withdrawal from society), his feasting with publicans and sinners and supplying wine for wedding celebrations indicate that his was not a life of ascetic spiritual withdrawal from society. While he chased the money changers out of the temple courtyards, suggesting an affinity with the Pharisees, who wished to protect the integrity of temple rites, his repeated chastisements of the pharisaical hypocrisy clearly antagonized that community. And when he advocated accommodation to the Romans ("Pay Caesar what is due to Caesar"), he seemed sympathetic to the compromises established between Rome and the Sadducees, only later to repudiate them for their lack of religious orthodoxy.

Christ belonged to no political party. In that sense, his kingdom clearly was not of this world. Yet at the same time, that kingdom was proclaimed to be present among his followers. The question was, therefore, how the kingdom of God related to the kingdoms of men which were still everywhere to be found.

Thus, the early church had little direction in terms of what path it should take in reconciling the demands of God's kingdom with the kingdoms of men. But even more important for later generations of Christians to realize is that not only did the early church have few guidelines within which to develop a social and political ethic, but also that the early church itself did little in the way of trying to develop a systematic social or political philosophy.

The reasons for this neglect were several. *First,* it must be remembered that the early Christian community was viewed by the Gentile world as a sect of a strange Near Eastern religion. As such, Christians were a minority of a minority—hardly in a position to pontificate on the social and political policies of the Roman Empire! The early church was so insignificant, politically speaking, that to engage in social or political action would have been an exercise in futility. There was, therefore, no practical need for the church to develop a social and political theory.

Second, the early Christians were primarily from the lower end of the socioeconomic spectrum. Hence, they were removed even one step further from the possibility of achieving significant political influence, above and beyond the problems associated with their minority status in the context of the Roman Empire.

Third, the early church's conviction that the return of Christ was at hand created pressures within the Christian community to concentrate almost exclusively on the direct evangelization of the world—sometimes to the extent of being imprudent in terms of providing for the exigencies of daily life. Thus in Second Thessalonians, Paul warns against those Christians who have apparently ceased to work in the expectation that the Lord's return would occur shortly. In the context of such expectations, we can understand why the early Christian community could find little need to develop a longitudinal philosophy of history together with its social and political implications.

Fourth, one must not forget that the relationship between the citizen and the state in the Roman Empire was essentially passive. There was no mass democracy with competing political parties in the sense which we now know it. And as opportunity for direct citizen involvement in the affairs of the empire was quite limited, so, too, was the need to develop a theory which might guide Christians participating in such endeavors.

Thus, all these factors combined give us a New Testament which generally speaks only incidentally and obliquely to questions of the state. There are a few exceptions, such as Romans 13, which speak of government as having been ordained of God and thereby rightfully receiving obedience. But this teaching is offset by Revelation 13, which speaks of government as having become corrupted into the power of Antichrist! So long as the church was not in a position to affect affairs of state in the first place, and so long as its interpretation of Christ's imminent return was such that historical consciousness could not emerge, the development of a practical political ethic was unnecessary. But as the church grew from a scattered minority to the officially sanctioned and sustained religion of the Roman Empire in a period of four hundred years, and as it acknowledged that

Christ's return might be yet many years into the future, the need for a political ethic to serve as a guide for Christians now bearing responsibility in the empire was enormous. It was to this situation that St. Augustine so brilliantly addressed himself.

In his *City of God* (412–426), St. Augustine divided all mankind into two groups. The one was "the city of man," which was the association of all individuals for whom self-love was the motivating principle of life. The other was "the city of God," which was the association of all individuals for whom the love of God was the motivating principle of life. The two cities, argued Augustine, were in perpetual conflict insofar as their basic motivations were antithetical.

Both cities physically occupy the same earthly territory, and thus those who are of the city of God may still be said to be in the city of man. And while the city of man is alien to the city of God, it nonetheless fulfills a very important purpose in God's providential care over the world. For due to man's rebellion against God and the substitution of love of self for the love of God, the state provides an ordering mechanism to prevent selfish men from destroying one another. In this context of order, the city of God is allowed to grow and prosper.

In some respects, Augustine's social theory is similar to that of Thomas Hobbes. Hobbes argued that man is by nature nasty, brutish, and antisocial. Only through the creation of a state can the war of all against all be halted. The fundamental difference between Hobbes and Augustine is that while Hobbes sees this condition as natural to man, Augustine sees this conflict as the result of the "fallenness" of man.

While this is a significant point of difference, the practical applications of both theories are strikingly similar. Man is not a social creature—but antisocial. The state is not natural to man—but it is necessary to protect him from self-destruction. The chief purpose of the state is not to pursue justice—but to create some semblance of order.

What is important to note at this point is that Augustine could have pursued quite a different argument. He might have suggested that the state is the outgrowth of the social instinct implanted in the nature of man at creation. He might have emphasized the words of the apostle Paul in Romans 13 suggesting that the state is an instrumentality for goodness and justice. Instead of emphasizing the points of tension between the city of man and the city of God, he might have emphasized the shared natural revelation between them in which both share some common areas of moral responsibility. (See, for example, Paul's argument in Romans 1 and 2.)

But the net impact of Augustinian political ethics nonetheless remains. It suggests that the most we can hope for in the state is order. It suggests that the state is fundamentally alien to human nature—and, of course, unnecessary to those who are truly members of the city of God. Augustinianism creates an aura of moral pessimism in which it is difficult to create visions of a better society or inspire men to work toward justice.

Evangelicals have been slow to free themselves from the limitations imposed by the Augustinian social theory. Undoubtedly, a reason for this has been that most of the modern critics of Augustine have attacked not only his social philosophy, but also his concepts of sin, human depravity, and divine grace. But one need not deny the universality of sin, the depravity of man, or their impact on interpersonal relations to take a more moderate position on the nature of the state, the sociability of human nature, or abiding universal norms of justice than does Augustine. But what happens altogether too often is that evangelicals baptize the American experience, which is so conducive to a negative view of the state, with theological justifications drawn from their Augustinian heritage. And once that happens, one is judged to be heretical if he deviates from the party line.

Pietism

A third factor which has strongly influenced evangelical social ethics is its pietist heritage. Pietism per se was a movement reacting against a purely confessional test for religious orthodoxy. Beginning in the late seventeenth century and of major importance in the eighteenth century, the pietist movement emphasized the importance of religious feeling and experience as opposed to the practices of the state churches, which seemingly insisted only on an intellectual assent to confessions of faith. Pietism is in some respects anti-institutional, stressing the spirit of the relationship between believers and their Lord as opposed to the form it takes. Thus, spontaneous prayers replace written prayers. Gospel songs and choruses replace traditional hymnody and liturgy. And testimonials replace creedal confessions.

The pietist influence received impetus in the United States through massive immigration of "Free church" dissenters, and it was reinforced by frontier evangelism, where Christians moved west ahead of the institutionalized churches of confessional Protestantism. In the twentieth century, evangelicals within the main-line confessional denominations were literally driven into the pietist Free churches because, strangely enough, there was greater faithfulness to confessional orthodoxy in the pietist movement than in the main-line confessional churches themselves.

The pietist influence has made some vital contributions to the health of American evangelicalism. Its tendency to disdain established rite and ritual has given evangelicals greater flexibility in testing new modes of mission and worship than has been true in the confessional churches. And the pietist insistence that we believe in God with our hearts as well as our heads encourages evangelicals to develop a Christian experience which involves more than simply the verbal confession of an historical creed.

But there have been drawbacks to the pietist influence in evangelicalism as well. Religious feeling, for example, is often used as the supreme test of religious commitment. Hence, the need to create a vigorous intellectual apologetic for the Christian faith is downgraded. In the area of social and political ethics, the importance of systematic inquiry into the causes and solutions of social and political problems is brushed away.

The net impact of this situation is that evangelical Christianity often takes on an anti-intellectual cast. Its social and political ethic, rather than being clearly thought out and systematically stated, is a collection of moralisms which tends to romanticize concrete social and political problems as if they were nothing more than vaguely "spiritual" in character.

Thus, Billy Graham addresses the problem of race relations and integration, and states: "Though the race question has important social implications, it is fundamentally a moral and spiritual issue. Only moral and spiritual approaches can provide a solution."[7] And Leighton Ford suggests: "Our greatest need is for an inner revolution that can transform men's hearts. . . . Moral aspirins and political pills cannot solve our problem. What we need is radical surgery for cancer of the soul."[8] In reference to the problem of the national energy crisis, Ford suggests that what is of greater importance is the crisis in moral power: "Today we are suffering from a widespread moral power failure, and a great portion of man's life is crippled because of a breakdown in our spiritual transformers!"[9] Speaking on the balance of payments problem, Ford suggests that "Moral deflation is a far greater problem for the free world today than monetary inflation. The moral drain is more critical than the gold drain."[10]

There is a degree of truth in each of these statements. But the point remains that simply converting men to Christianity does *not* solve the social and political problems of institutionalized racism, the energy crisis, or the balance of payments! Perhaps what is most needed in the evangelical community is a little more moral humility and a little less spiritual pride. One does not have to be a social historian to recognize that the Christian faith has not provided simple formulas for achieving the most efficient development of natural resources or balancing conflicting economic interests between "free traders" and "protectionists." Indeed, the very fact that evangelical ministers are usually forbidden by their congregations to deal with social and political matters from the viewpoint of Christian convictions (other than in moralistic terms) gives testimony to this fact. So long as evangelicals engage, then, in prescribing only moral clichés to difficult social and political problems, they are in fact avoiding any direct interrelating of their faith with the sociopolitical world around them. We forget that the early church experienced tremendous tension between Jewish and Gentile believers over the issue of fellowship between Christians of different ethnic groups. (See Acts 11 and 15.) The apostles themselves were so divided over who should succeed Judas to their brotherhood that they finally resolved the issue by casting lots! Accepting God's grace in Christ does not provide us with an easy set of answers to social, economic, or political questions. God's grace justifies us before the creator God—but it doesn't provide instant sanctification in dealings with our fellowman.

Gnosticism

There is a bit of irony in suggesting that the evangelical community, which takes such great pride in its attempted defense of orthodoxy, is itself guilty of heresy. Gnosticism was the first major heretical threat to the orthodoxy of the Christian confession; and, as we shall see, it is still with us.

There were numerous Gnostic sects in the first three centuries of the church's history. Many of these revolved around the teachings of prophetic figures who claimed affinity with the Christian community. Generally, the Gnostics held to a dualistic view of the universe in which the struggle between the forces of good and evil was a struggle between spirit and matter. The implications of this dualism were, of course, devastating to anybody who took the claims of the incarnation seriously. The Gnostics maintained that Christ was not made of flesh, but was a spirit who "appeared" to be flesh. A Christian view of the world which suggested that God had created the world and found it "good" was obviously alien to Gnostic logic, and to suggest that one could serve God by making his body a temple of the Lord was nothing short of preposterous. To the Gnostic, anything of the world was either illusory or evil. The trick was to escape the world of flesh and to free one's "spirit" for communion with God. (The term "gnostic" refers to the "gnosis" or "knowledge" passed on within the sect which teaches how this escape is accomplished.)

The Apostles' Creed, among others, was written largely in response to the threat that Gnostic teachings posed for Christian orthodoxy. The affirmations that God created the world, that Christ was born of a virgin, that his body was raised from the dead, and that there will be a future bodily resurrection of the dead for all believers—all of these were upholding the physical reality of the incarnation.

The early Gnostics did not deny the world of the spirit; they denied the world of the flesh. They did not deny the possibility of uniquely inspired sacred writings; to the contrary, they added to the canon writings of their own which they held to be of sacred value. And the Gnostics did not deny the supernatural or the miraculous; to the contrary, they claimed hosts of miraculous proofs for the truth of their beliefs.

Contemporary attacks on orthodoxy have been inspired by an almost complete opposite of Gnosticism. Since the seventeenth century, attacks on Christian orthodoxy have been based not on a denial of the physical, but on a denial of the spiritual; not on the basis of additional sacred writings, but on the repudiation of any uniquely inspired written source of revelation; not on the basis of miraculous proofs, but on the repudiation of any concept of the supernatural or miraculous whatever.

In responding to these attacks by the modern world, evangelical apologetics have tended to "spiritualize" or "gnosticize" Christian teachings. In an effort to defend the supernatural, they have tended to downgrade the natural. In an effort to defend revelation, they have tended to downgrade reason or natural theology. In an attempt to defend the uniqueness of sacred writ, they have tended to divorce it from the social and historical heritage from which it emerged. The net effect of this defense is to preach salvation in Christ as spiritual redemption, neglecting the physical aspects of that redemption as it plays itself out in the social and political world. Evangelicals have preached "justification" before God without having defined what "justice" is in the first place.

Thus, even the "neo-evangelicals," who lament the tendency of conservatives to divorce the gospel from real life, are prone to suggest that at least the evangelical community has not abandoned the "heart of the gospel message." Or they suggest that while Christianity does indeed relate to the whole of life and that the church has a mission to address the gospel to all dimensions of human existence, the "primary task" of the church is still to preach the gospel. Nowhere is there the recognition that the very gospel, as perceived in the evangelical community, is itself but half the gospel. In reacting to the immanental theologies of the modern world, the evangelical community has responded with a mystical gnosticism of its own, having abandoned any attempts at reaching toward a genuinely transcendental theology which both reconciles and overcomes the polarizing tendencies of each of the other alternatives.

Thus, evangelicals suggest that one can have a "saving knowledge of Christ" if he accepts spiritual salvation and redemption apart from whether or not he properly understands the earthly and fleshly consequences of that faith. But at the same time, the evangelical is unwilling to suggest that a theological liberal who understands the immanental consequences of Christian faith in the flesh can find salvation apart from reconciling his spirit to the creator God through Jesus Christ the mediator. Let's call a spade a spade. Half the gospel is half the gospel. Neither half alone is truly a saving gospel, at least not in the way that God intended.

It must be granted that much of the reason for this tendency in the evangelical community has been the attempt on its part to combat the heresy of the liberal theologians. But one does not combat heresy with heresy, just as one does not right a lie with another lie.

But I suspect that there has been another reason for the tendency to gnosticize the gospel on the part of the evangelical community. Whereas in the effort to combat heresy at least the motivations of the evangelicals were pure, in this case the motivations themselves are suspect. Evangelicals are, by and large, very comfortable in terms of their socioeconomic position. And any gospel which takes seriously either the Old Testament or the New Testament injunctions to care for the poor and to free oneself of materialist concerns is a hard pill to swallow. How desperately we need to hear the words of James: "Next a word to you who have great possessions. Weep and wail over the miserable fate descending on you" (James 5:1). The suburban captivity of the church has fostered the political captivity of the Christians.

Each of these factors—individualism, negativism toward the state, pietism, and Gnosticism—serve to mutually support one another. If one assumes that social problems are really only compounded individual problems, then it is only logical to hold to a negative view of the state. After all, the state can't really do anything that people can't do for themselves. Or if one begins with a negative view of the state, he will obviously be inclined to seek individualist rather than statist solutions to social problems. Individualism and the negative view of the state are then further reinforced by a pietist view of life which refuses to face the intellectual shortcomings of this position. It turns to the heart and romantic notions of community in Christ as a community in which all disagreements have ceased. (One need look only at the New Testament and church history to gather quite a different picture!) Pietism fails to see that justification in Christ does not bring about some sort of instant sanctification in the relations between men. And it fails to answer the problem of how Christians are to balance their demands with those of non-Christians in the world community. Finally, succumbing to a Gnostic concept of salvation and moral obligation, the evangelical community has tended to dismiss its critics as having misunderstood the essentially "spiritual" character of the Christian gospel.

The ethical consequences of this situation are well known. Evangelicals have concerned themselves with individual sin, individual repentance, and individual renewal. They have addressed themselves forcefully to the problems of drugs, alcohol, lust, and personal example in interpersonal relations. But evangelicals have failed to deal with corporate sin, corporate repentance, and corporate renewal. This is obvious to the outside observer. But the evangelical finds it difficult to see the truth or gravity of the charge made against him. For if all problems are viewed as essentially individual problems, then addressing oneself to individual morality has *ipso facto* solved the problem of social morality.

Obviously there is some merit in the evangelical's argument that as individuals are changed, the world is changed. The question is, however, *how* does one change individuals? Is it a matter of individuals changing themselves (with God's help)? What if some individuals resist change? Is moral improvement thereby out of the question? Can a majority in society set standards for the entire society? If we cannot legislate genuine morality, can we not at least legislate external behavior between individuals in society? It is at this point that the evangelical's answer to social and political problems has been haphazard and inconsistent. We are told that one can't legislate against racism. But at the same time we are encouraged to support laws against drugs, alcohol, and sexual promiscuity. We are told that new gun-control laws won't get at the heart of crime. But at the same time we are told that capital punishment and mandatory incarceration for certain crimes rest on biblical principle.

Because evangelical ethics are rooted more in the political heritage of seventeenth- and eighteenth-

their romantic pietism, and their spiritualized concepts of salvation, they are unable to speak to the
need for *political* solutions for *social* problems in
historical existence. We need more than penance for
sins of the past. What is needed is a fundamental—
even elemental—discussion of the nature of man,
society, and politics from an evangelical perspective.
Once this basic groundwork is laid, steps can be
taken toward developing strategies for social and
political engagement.

The Nature of Man and Society

What is the nature and destiny of man? Only as we
give answer to this can we answer the question,
"What is the nature and function of politics?" For
politics, in the last analysis, must be seen as a part of
man's attempt to find meaning and purpose within
his historical existence. Thus, at the very beginning
we see that politics receives its definition and
function from our view of man. Here the great
biblical teachings of the evangelical tradition may be
seen to touch at the heart of everything we shall say
subsequently about the political world.

The evangelical confesses that man is a being
qualitatively different from any other of God's
creation. According to the Genesis creation account,
man is the capstone of God's creation, and he shares
in the very image of God. Sharing in God's image, he
is therefore capable of having fellowship and communion with God. Further, he may be said to share
to some extent in the very attributes of God—self-
transcendence, freedom, and creative power. God

charged man with establishing dominion over the earth, and thus in some ways man mirrors God's sovereignty over the universe through his own assigned sovereignty over the earth. Finally, man was created to live not only with God, but also with his fellowman. God did not create man to be alone, but to be in the company of other persons, all sharing equally in their fundamental distinction from any other product of God's creation: the image of God implanted in man.

But man attempted to assert his God-given likeness beyond the limits set by the Creator. Created in God's image to live in creative freedom, man used his powers to challenge the freedom and sovereignty of God himself. Thus man was cursed by God for having marred the image of God itself. The harmony of parts creating an ordered relationship between man, his fellowman, and God the Creator was destroyed.

Man may thus be said to live a schizophrenic existence. His existential selfhood (what he has become) is perpetually at conflict with his created essence (what he was created to be). His consciousness of the ordered relationships which ought to exist between himself, God, and his fellowman constantly hurls itself against the fact that he has been sent away from the Garden in which God first placed him.

But the image of God in man remains, and God does not forsake man. Man may continually abuse that image and continually set himself against the Creator, but God constantly calls man back to his intended purpose and created nature through acts of goodness and mercy, chastisement and judgment. Through these acts and the testimonies of divine creation, all men still experience the sacredness of their nature and the capacity for communion with God and their fellowman.

Thus, man the sinner does not suddenly become an asocial animal capable of no moral good. Were that the case, man would no longer be morally responsible to either God or his fellowman. Rather, God sustains man. He places limits on the powers of evil. Man remains a being bearing the image of God. He still hears the voice of God when God approaches him. He retains some capacity to fulfill freely the purposes for which he was created in God's image. Because all men share in this capacity, there remains a point of contact and commonness which allows the essentially social nature of man to find expression.

To say that the image of God remains in man is not to say that the image has not been marked and marred by sin. But if the image of God were obliterated, that being which we call man would no longer truly be man. To say that man can still hear the voice of God is not to say that man will listen to the voice of God. But if man could no longer hear the voice of God, he would no longer be man. To say that man is capable of doing moral good is not to say that man is capable of earning merit justifying himself before God. But if man is incapable of any moral good, he cannot be held morally responsible.

These are fine distinctions which are often overlooked by evangelicals in their zeal to combat the exaltation of man by modern liberal humanism. The liberals have often tended to deny that man is a fallen creature. Evangelicals have tended to counter that man is nothing more than a fallen creature. Both miss the critical balance of recognizing that while man is a fallen creature, he nonetheless continues to bear the image of God. The liberals have exalted man's capacity for good to the point that they suggest man can earn salvation. The evangelicals have emphasized man's capacity for evil to the point that man is no longer seen as capable of any good. Both miss the critical balance of recognizing that man still has moral responsibility and capacity to choose for either good or evil. In choosing evil he simply compounds the terrors of a disordered life, and in choosing good he acts to bring life back into harmony with the Word—the very Word which tells him that there is no remission for sin aside from God's sacrifice of himself. The liberals have tended to exalt the social nature of man into a panacea for overcoming all selfishness. The evangelicals have tended to view the selfishness of man as an obstacle to achieving any genuine society. Both miss the critical balance of recognizing that man is a social creature by creation and God's sustaining grace despite the fact that he chooses to exalt self above both God and his fellowman.

The liberal, while recognizing that man is fallen, still sees him capable of achieving his own redemption. Christ is but a prototype of the potential for goodness in all men. If this view is extended to its logical conclusion, then, all men, in fact, can become

very God of very God. The consequences of this
approach for social theory are obvious. Man's
inability to reenter the garden of peace is self-
inflicted. But by using his creative powers and
turning freely to do the good, man can establish a
perfect society which has overcome all evil. Liberals
differ radically, of course, on the means of pursuit,
their identification of the sources of good and evil,
and the immediacy by which they think their goals
can be met. But since all men share in the commonness of God-likeness, all men are equal in the
resources essential to the reestablishment of social
harmony and a just society. Society and the state are
therefore rooted in a natural ethic known to all men.

The evangelical has reacted strongly against the
almost flippant attitude that the liberal manifests in
regard to the problem of man's fall into sin. The
danger has been in overreacting to the point that
man's "total depravity" is construed to mean that
man is capable of no good whatever. Rather than
viewing man as bearing the likeness of God, the
evangelical reminds himself that as man was created
from dust, so shall he return to dust again. In
reaction to the liberal's humanistic understanding of
Christ and his deification of man, the evangelical has
so emphasized the deity of Christ that he seems blind
to the humanness of Christ, and he has so under-
valued the potential of man that he seems blind to
the *imago dei* rooted in man. The consequences of
this confusion for social theory are likewise obvious.

According to this evangelical view, man can do
nothing to reenter the garden of peace. He deludes

himself when thinking that he acts creatively or freely—he is really captive to the powers of evil. Strategies of social reform and renewal are secondary to and dependent upon the more basic question of how man can escape the pervasiveness of sin. Only in finding individual salvation can one find the path to social salvation. But since all men are alienated from God and each other through sin, there can be no really cooperative endeavor toward reestablishing social harmony and justice apart from the redemptive action of God in Christ Jesus. The state and society are thus, in this evangelical view, rooted in a uniquely revealed ethic resting on the redemptive power of God known only to those to whom God has chosen to show himself.

For the liberal, politics is based on a natural ethic rooted in man's divinity as a created being. For the evangelical, politics is based on a revealed ethic rooted in Christ's redemptive power. The liberal therefore sees the possibility of an inclusive political base joining together both the believer and the nonbeliever united by their common humanity. Such an approach can be rationally perceived, and man has within himself the ability to construct healthy political societies based on this ethic. The evangelical, on the other hand, sees mankind hopelessly divided into factions—the most fundamental being that between the redeemed and the unredeemed. These two cannot really work together because their ethics are based on fundamentally different conceptions of the nature of man and the foundations for society.

What is desperately needed is a via media between these two extremes. What is needed is an ethic which recognizes that all men still bear the image of God and thereby possess the capacity for an inclusive society based on natural ethics and at the same time recognizes that man's fall into sin places fundamental limitations on the success of such an endeavor. What is needed is an ethic which recognizes that God's redemptive power in Christ holds the key to the ultimate success of social and political reconciliation, but at the same time recognizes that God still sustains the prerequisites necessary for an at least rudimentary success at the social and political level. The liberal fails to see that a purely humanist politics is forever doomed because man is a sinner. The evangelical fails to see that a purely redemptionist politics is a contradiction in terms. For redemption, when viewed as a totally accomplished fact, obliviates the need for politics. But to understand this, we must now change our focus to the nature of politics itself.

The Nature of Politics

Because all men have tasted sin, all men share in the consequences of sin. All men consequently elevate the love of self above their love of God or fellowman. That perfect society balancing the love of self, love of one's brother, and love of God which the Creator had intended has been upset. Discord has usurped the harmonious relations between the parts. Self-interest asserts itself over the interests of God and our fellowman.

Politics is simply the means men use to ameliorate the conflicts stemming from this situation. Man finds himself trapped in moral anarchy. But because he is a social being by creation, this anarchy is intolerable to him. He seeks accords with his fellowman which are in keeping with his self-interest. Failing that, he resorts to force and violence to assert his self-interest over the interests of others.

Conflict stemming from self-interest must therefore be seen to lie at the heart of politics. Were there no conflict, there would be no need for politics. Political society, as opposed to what we might call "natural" society, is itself a consequence of sin. Were there no sin, there would be no selfishness. Were there no selfishness, there would be no conflict. And were there no conflict, there would be no need for politics.

In order to pursue their self-interests, individuals associate with others who share the same interests. Thus, interest groups and political parties are established to promote and pursue certain interests. But even within these associations, conflicts of interest emerge between the members as to tactics to be employed and the ranking of priorities.

It is of utmost importance to recognize that conflict is integral to politics. Both liberals and evangelicals have generally tended to try to escape this fact. Liberals try to romanticize conflict away by euphemistically insisting that since men are essentially brothers, they share essentially the same interests. Hence, the purpose of politics is to strip away the veneer of apparent conflict and create a peaceful society based on shared, common interest. This fails to recognize the utter pervasiveness of sin which extends to the very root of the human heart and all human relationships.

The evangelicals, on the other hand, have also tried to escape the fact that conflict is integral to politics. They tend to see conflict as in itself evil, rather than seeing it as a by-product of evil. Therefore, conflict is to be avoided—and if not avoided, at least denied. The evangelical all too often longs for a politics devoid of conflict—a contradiction in terms. Evangelicals generally argue that political conflict would be resolved if all parties to the conflict were reconciled to God. But they fail to recognize that we live in a world where all individuals are not likely to seek such reconciliation. And they fail to recognize that conflicts continue even among the members of God's household. For regeneration in Christ does not completely sanctify relations between men. Conflicts continue to exist—for man continues to sin.

Conflict is integral to politics. So is consensus. Conflict is a consequence of the ego centeredness of man resulting from the Fall. Conflict makes politics necessary. Consensus is the product of man's ability to reach beyond pure self-interest. Consensus makes politics possible. Conflict without consensus would result in pure egoism—social anarchy. Consensus without conflict would cease to be politics—it would be a natural harmony, a return to the garden of peace.

Once again, both liberals and evangelicals have

rather simplistic notions as to how consensus can be achieved. To the liberal, consensus can be found rather easily by making moral appeals to man's capacity for idealism and self-transcendence. To the evangelical, consensus is viewed as an automatic by-product of man's reunion with God. The liberal fails to understand that man's selfishness is never totally separate from his idealism. The evangelical fails to understand that his reconciliation with God not only establishes new social division within the human community (redeemed v. unredeemed), but that it can also create a righteous zeal detrimental to the practice of politics. For "true believers" of any stripe are always tempted to become hard-core ideologues seeking to impose their truths on society at large. The more firmly they hold on to their truths, the less willing they often are to compromise them in the political arena.

Political consensus is really a polite term for political compromise. All politics involves compromising the conflicts of interest within a society. Political institutions and traditions are nothing more than the channels through which the conflicts are routed and the rules by which the conflicts are fought. No political consensus—the reaching of an accord between opposing political conflicts—is equally advantageous to all the players. There are always those who are relatively the winners and relatively the losers. Political compromise never puts an end to political conflict. It simply changes the terms and the relative advantages and disadvantages the players have in the pursuit of their interests.

Because politics is a never-ending cycle of conflict seeking consensus, moralists of all stripes become quickly frustrated. They seek absolute answers of eternal significance as opposed to the calculated compromises of politics. They tend to do one of two things. Either they become political extremists seeking to impose their self-assured truths on society in the effort to establish the grand and final solution to social conflict, or they withdraw from political life because they refuse to taint themselves with compromise.

But the ability to accept compromise is the mark of political maturity. It is the very stuff out of which politics is made. Purist ideological crusades and ascetic withdrawal must both be seen as the acts of sophomoric arrogance, which they are.

To elevate compromise as a principle of politics is not to insist that all political values or all political interests are equally meritorious. Nor is it to suggest that all truth is relative and that all political solutions are therefore relative. But no one man or party—or even a majority of an entire national population—ever has a pure, unadulterated grasp of truth. While truth is not relative, man's grasp of it is. Compromise in politics is necessary because man's political ambitions never totally transcend his selfishness. Indeed, we have more to fear from the ideological purist who dresses his demands in robes of white than the practical realist who openly confesses the personal interests attached to his political demands. To insist that one has the perfect solution to a political problem is to commit a sin of

immense personal pride as well as to reveal a parochialism of understanding.

Withdrawal from politics is as morally reprehensible as is an attack on all politics from the standpoint of ideological purity. When men compete for political goals, implicit in their actions are ethical assumptions pertaining to the good. One person works to achieve change because he believes change will be for the better. Or another opposes change because he believes change will be for the worse. All politics demands ethical commitment. In the last analysis, all politics is then a struggle between competing conceptions of the good—or, if you will, between good and evil.

One cannot, therefore, withdraw from this struggle without affecting a net change in the balance of power between competing political interests. To withdraw is in essence to capitulate, if not to evil, at least to what one perceives to be a lesser vision of the good. Such withdrawal is an abdication of moral responsibility. How ironic, then, that those who do withdraw from politics often rationalize their actions by insisting that politics is a dirty business and they want to keep their hands clean!

But is politics a dirty business? Certainly the withdrawal of those sharing Christian standards from meaningful participation in political life does little to help the situation. But despite the fact that this often happens, one cannot say that politics in and of itself is either good or evil. Political decisions reflect the nature of the inputs or demands which are brought to bear on the political decision-making

process. Politics is but a tool which can have consequences for good or evil. But the cause of the good is not helped when political demands sensitive to God's Word are no longer heard. For then half a loaf becomes none. And the entire political system suffers to an even greater extent from spiritual starvation.

The Moral Ambiguity of Politics

We have suggested above that all political activity is involved in the struggle between good and evil. But at the same time, in the world of politics, it is always extremely difficult to say with certainty what is good and what is bad. Politics is surrounded by problems of moral ambiguity.

We have, for example, argued that politics is always an exercise in self-interest. No political endeavor completely transcends the egoism of its supporters. Hence, all politics are partially rooted in selfishness. How, then, does a Christian reconcile political activity with his calling to live a life in conformity to Jesus Christ? We have also argued that all political decisions involve compromises in the search for a politically workable consensus. Politics seeks to find common ground amidst diverse demands, none of which is perfectly pure or righteous to begin with. Politics, then, always demands compromise with evil. The question is not whether or not evil will be mixed with the good, but rather whether and to what degree we will be conscious of the evil involved in our actions. How, then, can the Christian actively pursue compromise

in the political world without compromising his own faithfulness to demands God makes on him to live a life of righteousness?

By way of general introduction to this problem, let us remember that politics is not the only aspect of life in which moral ambiguity is present. What distinguishes politics is the *extent* of moral ambiguity, not the simple fact of its presence. The businessman faces morally ambiguous decisions when he negotiates between the demands of labor for higher wages and benefits and the demands of stockholders for larger dividends and capital investment. Both parties often have right on their side. Yet neither side is free of selfish interest. The church faces morally ambiguous decisions in deciding how to budget its resources amidst legitimate demands for staff salaries, building funds, evangelism, and charity. The parents of school children face morally ambiguous decisions between quality education for their own children or, perhaps, an education of lesser quality for their own children, but an education of better quality for the population at large through forced racial integration.

The problem of moral ambiguity is often easier for the liberal to handle than for the conservative, evangelical Christian. The liberal is often willing to accept the concept of contextual morality. He often denies the existence of absolute, objective moral norms. If right and wrong are themselves relative, there is no difficulty in accepting a contextual morality which adjusts itself to the exigencies of the moment. (The irony in all this for the liberal is that he so often engages in moral crusades. How can he justify his sense of moral indignation and outrage over matters which are only relatively just or unjust?)

But the problem of moral ambiguity poses a much greater dilemma to the evangelical who subscribes to an infallible and eternal Word which establishes absolute standards for human behavior. Since right and wrong are absolute, how can one accept compromise or change one's standards to meet the needs of the moment? (Of course, there is irony here as well, for the evangelical, who is so often cocksure of the existence of absolute moral standards, is generally unwilling to engage in prophetic judgment upon society because he sees these standards as being so difficult to relate to specific issues that he is left speechless. Of what use are the standards?)

There are at least three dimensions to the problem of moral ambiguity in politics which must be recognized. The *first* dimension pertains to the problem of establishing absolute ethical foundations for political action. What is desperately needed is the moral humility to accept the fact that while God's standards are absolute and unchanging, we as individuals are never able to know or apply them with perfection. For all our talk to the contrary, we in the evangelical community have taken the concept of sin too lightly! While God has shown us what he wants, our obedience is always affected by what we are willing to see and do in response to his revelation. And even what we do—we might add—is by the grace of God, lest we should boast of our moral superiority!

Further, we pointed out in the previous chapter that the New Testament, in particular, generally speaks only obliquely about the problems of politics. For since political activity was not an option for the early Christian community, there was little need to discuss it. Hence, our guides to political action are based to a great degree on church tradition and our cultural history, not on direct biblical guidelines. If orthodox Christians practicing charity toward one another cannot come to agreement on matters where there appears to be direct biblical teaching (such as the administration of the sacraments or eschatology), it can hardly be expected that they will come to agreement on those matters where biblical teachings are arrived at only indirectly and inductively.

It is important, however, to keep the distinction in mind between the relativist who insists that truth is simply relative, and the moral absolutist who questions not the existence of moral absolutes but rather the limitations of man's ability to grasp moral truth in its entirety.

The *second* dimension of moral ambiguity in politics pertains to the very complicated problems with which politics must deal. Not only do we have an incomplete understanding of the ethical foundations of political action, but also we have an incomplete understanding of the facts upon which ethical decisions must be based. In addition, the facts themselves are always subject to change since social conditions are never static but always in a state of flux and change. Hence, individuals who share

similar moral perspectives on issues will often
advocate differing policies because they disagree on
the facts pertaining to a political question.

Such instances can be illustrated easily. Senator
Barry Goldwater voted against the 1964 Civil Rights
Act not because he disagreed with the intent of the
legislation, but because he believed it to be uncon-
stitutional. Many conservative Christians supported
legislation requiring health warnings on cigarette
packages and restricting television advertising of
cigarettes. Others equally concerned about the ill
effect of cigarette smoking opposed this legislation
as a dangerous precedent of government regulation
of trade and commerce. Many religious leaders
oppose the establishment of state-run lotteries
because they are against gambling on principle and
the social hardships it often creates for those in the
lower classes who are prone to gamble heavily. Other
religious leaders, however, equally opposed to the
evils of gambling, support state-run lotteries as a
means of undercutting the financial bonanza that
illegal gambling provides for organized crime. Some
religious leaders oppose liberalized abortion laws.
Others, equally opposed to abortion, support
liberalized abortion laws because they don't believe
one ought to "legislate morality" or that one can
moralize about the rights of the unborn until one
shows equal compassion and concern about the
rights of those already born. Many political leaders
are concerned about the concentration of political
power in the national government. Others are just as
equally concerned, but see no alternative to the

problem unless state and local governments prove themselves able to exercise their powers wisely. Thus, moral agreement—as rare as it may be in politics—does not guarantee political harmony.

The *third* dimension of moral ambiguity in political decision making pertains to the unintended consequences of political actions. Two parties may share the same moral concerns and outlook. They may also be agreed in their assessments of a factual situation. They may even agree that a particular problem will be solved by a particular program of government action. But they may disagree vigorously over the unintended consequences of government action.

Both liberals and conservatives in Congress may support the concept of an all-volunteer army. They may both believe that military conscription is inconsistent with the concept of a free society. They may both believe that the concept of a volunteer army might be a sort of democratic check on the war-making powers of Congress and the president since the strength of the armed forces and the military capacity of the nation would in the future rest increasingly on the popular support of national military policy. Yet, one may still disagree with the proposal for an all-volunteer army since it might encourage a professional military elite to emerge, separated and insulated from main-line democratic values in the society. Another might disagree with the proposal on the basis that the military—now short of much needed manpower—will have to turn to a military strategy based increasingly on massive nuclear confrontation in place of the military strategy of conventional warfare which calls for large armies. In other words, one may very much favor a particular policy—but reject it nonetheless due to the possibility of unintended consequences.

This same principle also works in reverse. Individuals who do not share similar moral or factual assessments of a political situation may nonetheless support similar policy goals. A black person may not have opposed the war in Southeast Asia on moral grounds, but simply on the basis that it diverted national resources away from much needed domestic spending. A parent may not have opposed the war in Southeast Asia on principle, and may be equally opposed to increased spending for human resources on the domestic front, but still have wished the war's end for the simple reason that he didn't wish to see his son inducted into the armed forces. A businessman might have cared less about the war, or poverty, or the parent's child sent to Vietnam or Cambodia, but have opposed the war nonetheless because he was worried about inflation. Thus, for different reasons they supported the same policy. As the saying goes, "Politics makes strange bedfellows."

If Christians are to rise above political naiveté, they must begin by recognizing that political problems are immensely complex and clouded. And they must recognize that the motives behind political action are generally mixed. Hence, politics is not a simple battle between good and evil, or virtuous men and evil men.

However, we should be warned against the danger of using the moral ambiguity of politics as an excuse for moral agnosticism which refuses to speak to political issues. This is just as dangerous as a simplistic and absolute identification of the moral good with one's own pet political cause. While liberals have often identified God's cause with specific pieces of legislation or particular social movements, evangelicals have at the same time rationalized their own lack of social involvement by insisting that since the Bible doesn't speak *directly* to these issues, they themselves can say *nothing* about them.[2]

Our inability to come to a perfect understanding of God's will on political matters does not serve as an excuse for silence. Rather, it calls for humility and restraint. The Christian affirms that God has spoken and shown himself in Christ Jesus. Thus the Christian comes to the political world with insights and moral commitment which at least to a relative degree are capable of transcending the egoism of politics. While Christians ought not hope for perfect and complete political accord, they can at least seek out broad principles upon which to agree. After all, we do not cease in the effort to enunciate church dogma just because dogmatic statements fall short of perfection. Why, then, should we cease in the effort to enunciate Christian social principles just because they too fall short of perfection? The corrective for simplistic moral absolutizing in politics is not abstention, but recognizing the inherent limitations and moral ambiguity of the political world.

Political Justice

Thus far, our discussion of politics has been essentially descriptive. We have suggested that politics is the ongoing search for social consensus amidst a world of competing personal demands. But politics is something more than simply the struggle for personal advantage. It is the attempt of the entire society to organize and manipulate personal demands in such a way that the consensus which is reached will, insofar as possible, be fair to each member of that society. In other words, politics is intimately involved in man's search for justice.

But what is justice? The classic answer to this question throughout the ages has been: "Justice is rendering to every man his due." But what is every man's due? It may seem ironic that a question as fundamental as this cannot be answered with great precision. Justice, to paraphrase H. Emil Brunner, is like a straight line. We all have a concept of what a straight line ought to be, but nowhere does a perfectly straight line exist in factual reality.[3] As unsatisfactory as this analogy may seem, it is nonetheless essential that politics not lose sight of the concept of justice. For if we deny the existence of an abstract and transcendental notion of the political good, then the processes of politics can be reduced to nothing more than brute force asserting its will over a weaker party.

Virtually every civilization and society throughout history has at least paid lip service to the concept of political justice. By it is meant that notion of right or wrong which is implanted in the human heart pertaining to the legitimate distribution of the resources of the given society. (This notion is what theologians often refer to as God's "general revelation" to all people or what philosophers refer to as the "natural law" ethic.) All societies have the concept of law receiving legitimacy insofar as it is in accord with that sense of moral rightness in the minds of its citizens. Obviously, different societies at different points in time have had drastically differing concepts on the particular contents of this higher, universal moral law. But on the broad principle that moral standards exist and should be pursued, there has been a substantive agreement among all civilizations.[4]

In Romans 1 and 2, Paul refers to this moral law as evidence of the fact that God has not abandoned man to moral anarchy. God has provided, through his sustaining grace and general revelation, at least a minimal moral foundation for society which stands as a guide for all peoples. This understanding is of utmost importance for the Christian concerned with politics because it creates the basis for an ecumenical politics. That is, Christians and non-Christians can work together for the political good because all men—regardless of their relationship to Christ—share a degree of common moral unity.

Because each society faces the task of working out the particular content and application of abstract justice in the context of its own particular environment, it is extremely difficult to delineate the criteria of a just society at all specific points. However, history seems to have indicated the utility of at least four *instrumental* values useful in the search for this definition. By instrumental values, we mean certain goals which ought to underlie all political action in the search for justice.

The first of these instrumental values is that of *order*. When we speak of a just society, we are referring first of all to what we commonly call the "just political order." Because of the conflicts and ambiguities inherent in politics, it is necessary to establish institutions by which political conflicts can be regulated and society itself protected from anarchy. Hence, Romans 13 cites the fact that God himself approves of the institutional ordering of society as an instrument for achieving justice. If society has no institutionalized means for creating political order, then it has no means by which to pursue justice. Note, however, that order is an instrumental value and not an end in itself. Institutionalized political authority exists for the sake of pursuing the good. Should the government— as so often happens—become a terror to the good, it will have perverted itself into a beast. (See Revelation 13.)

The second instrumental value is that of *freedom*. By freedom we mean the right of self-expression and self-determination insofar as it is not incongruent with the legitimate restraints imposed upon in- dividuals for the sake of political order. As such, freedom must be distinguished from license, which may be defined as simply the absence of restraint.

Freedom and order must be balanced in any society. Yet they must not be seen as opposites.

Rather, they complement each other and neither can properly exist without the other. Freedom without order ceases to be freedom—it degenerates into anarchy and license. Order without freedom ceases to be order—it substitutes authoritarianism for authority. When in proper balance, both freedom and order are maximized.

The third instrumental value is that of *equality*. Political equality means that the political system will not make arbitrary discriminations against particular individuals or groups within a society. Of course, the question of what is "arbitrary" is an extremely difficult one. John Stuart Mill argued that citizens who owned land or had a university education should be allowed to cast two votes in national elections on the basis that landowners had a greater stake in the electoral outcome and educated individuals could make more informed choices. Hence, both should be allowed an extra vote. Is this reasonable or is it arbitrary? In the early years of the United States, only taxpaying landowners could vote since, it was argued, they were the ones which supported the burden of government financially. In recent years, the United States courts have upheld statutes which allow only landowners to vote in tax millage assessments since they alone pay for the tax directly. Are these reasonable or arbitrary restraints?

Further, the question of political equality—that is, the concept of dispassionate justice before the law—cannot be totally separated from the question of social equality or egalitarianism. Insofar as society is more than simply a contract between individuals seeking their own self-interest, the concept of equality must include a concept of equity in terms of the distribution of the resources of a society. But how the particulars of this value are to be delineated is just as ambiguous as trying to say once and for all what the perfect balance between the values of order and freedom ought to be.

The fourth instrumental value is that of *participation*. Participation in government decision making was held in such great value by theorists such as Plato, Aristotle, and Rousseau that they refused to conceive of a just political society other than that of a city-state in which all citizens could participate directly on a face-to-face basis. Concepts of mass participation via indirect representation have replaced the simple democracy of these earlier theorists. But they all agree that government must be accountable to the people, and that accountability is best achieved by allowing broad participation in the selection of leaders and determination of policies.

While the presence of these four instrumental values—order, freedom, equality, and participation—is not an adequate definition of a just society, it is safe to say that they will always be marks of a just society. But as we have seen, even in defining instrumental values, there is a great deal of ambiguity implicit in the search for justice.

Christian Insights on Justice

Some readers will be troubled with the preceding argument. First, one may ask why there was no attempt to define justice *substantively* as opposed to emphasizing only the instrumental values of justice. Second, one may ask why in dealing with the instrumental values of justice we refused to engage in precise descriptions of these instrumental values and emphasized again the ambiguity implicit therein. And third, one may ask whether or not the Christian revelation does not solve the moral ambiguity of justice and enable us to become more explicit and substantive in dealing with this problem. The first two of these questions can be answered rather briefly. The answer to the third question will take up most of this section.

In answer to the first question, the distinction between instrumental justice and substantive justice is ultimately an arbitrary one. To suggest otherwise is to believe that there is no integral relationship between political ends and the means used to pursue them. There is always the danger in politics that individuals can believe so strongly in the rightness of their cause that they will participate in unjust means to pursue what they believe to be a just end. In the process, the end itself becomes corrupted.

This problem, among others, was at the heart of the Watergate crisis. Some of President Nixon's supporters believed so strongly that his continued leadership was a political good that they violated the law (the basic institutional *order*ing of society) to pursue his reelection. In the process, the justice and rightness of his entire reelection and forthcoming administration were cast into doubt. In order to achieve their aims, they infringed on the civil *freedoms* of several noteworthy Americans, and in doing so raised the specter of a society in which freedom could be sacrificed if the end were only great enough. In retrospect, many Americans were left wondering whether the electoral procedures by which Americans *participate* in determining their leaders and national policies were so violated as to cast doubt on the legitimacy of the election itself. The crisis of Watergate was not that of defining substantive justice, but of violations of instrumental justice which called into question the legitimacy of any government policy or leader brought about by such means. Hence, means and ends cannot be separated.

Because the Watergate issue has received such widespread attention and because most thoughtful Americans have given it some serious consideration, the above may seem rather obvious. But if this principle applies in the case of Watergate, it must be seen to apply in other instances as well. It applies in the area of criminal justice where the means used to attack the problem of crime must be consistent with the ends. That is, one must not encourage the use of unlawful procedures in order to defend the law. The principle applies in cases of controlling civil disobedience and civil dissent where one must not violate constitutional rights to protect the Constitution. For once the instrumental values of justice are disregarded, substantive justice is reduced to the arbitrary definition of any party or individual successful in forcing its or his will on the masses by any means it chooses. This principle applies to Christians, as well, who are sometimes tempted to endorse policies because they believe them to be substantively correct while paying little regard to the means which might be used to pursue them. Prayers in public schools may be seen as just and good. (Here, of course, many Christians would disagree.) But one must not exalt those political leaders and educators who openly disregard Supreme Court rulings by encouraging prayers in public schools— for such unlawful disobedience only sets the precedent for others who might wish to pursue other goals outside of the law.

Second, we have refused to engage in precise definitions of the values of which instrumental justice is composed. We have done this because these values are strongly conditioned by the political and social environment of each culture. We have stated that political order is a characteristic of instrumental justice. But order always exists in a tandem relationship with the value of freedom. Different societies and cultures are comfortable with different balances between the two. The point to be remembered is that in no case must either freedom or order be exalted to the exclusion of the other.

Likewise, different cultural traditions vary tremendously in regard to the means and extent of participation in the political process. In Western democratic countries, we associate participation with the right to vote on candidates and policies at regular intervals. In traditional societies, the value of participation is mediated through a very stable culture which places constraints on the powers and policies of leaders even though formal electoral procedures do not exist. Thus, in an African tribe, the tribal chief makes his rulings on the basis of a sort of common law passed down within the tribe over hundreds of years. If he violates this law, he will lose his office. It is difficult for us to understand how such traditional restraints and mediated forms of participation are meaningful and effective. Yet in such cultures they are as meaningful and effective as our Western forms of participation. On the other hand, as the cultures change, it becomes imperative that the mode of participation change as well, just as our own modes of electoral participation have changed drastically from the days of a very restricted electorate to the use of mass politics today.

Finally, the concept of equality is strongly affected by cultural factors. Until only recently, women were not allowed to vote in Switzerland. And yet, few Westerners would thereby conclude that Switzerland was not an open, democratic society. Before the passage of the Twenty-sixth Amendment to the U.S. Constitution in 1971, giving the vote to all citizens of eighteen years of age or older, few felt that there was a fundamental problem in that some states allowed eighteen-year-old voting while others did not.

All of these factors—order, freedom, participation, and equality—must be considered on the basis of differing cultures within different political environments. Just as the Christian church universal differs significantly in its various liturgies, social taboos, etc., as they are defined in differing historical settings, so, too, we must expect the same in the political world.

However, our insistence on emphasizing the instrumental values of a just society—as opposed to dealing explicitly with a substantive definition of justice—together with our insistence on emphasizing the cultural relativity of these instrumental values leads to the third possible objection raised above. Does the Christian faith in the revealed Word of God not fill this void? Or are we left in a political world informed only by moral ambiguity and cultural relativism? In other words, is the Christian's ability to provide substantive and absolute moral values for social justice thoroughly mitigated by the moral ambiguity and cultural relativism through which he operates?

The answer to this question is both yes and no. The Christian is indeed in a unique position to give moral direction to the definition of justice insofar as he asserts that God's Word overcomes the moral ambiguity (or moral lostness of man estranged from God) of life with its revelation of God's standards of righteousness. On the other hand, as we pointed out earlier in this chapter, the pervasiveness of man's rebellion against God is such that in the process of utilizing God's revelation he tends to appropriate it for his own selfish purposes. The net effect, of course, is to relativize and demean God's absolute law.

However, while it is imperative that Christians recognize the dangers of moralizing self-interest under the cloak of God's Word, at the same time they must recognize that there is a fundamental difference between that of a simple moral relativism and that of a moral absolute perceived and acted upon imperfectly by confessing Christians. There are several reasons why this is so.

First, even though Christians can appropriate the absolute demands of God only on a relative basis, they are still at a relative advantage over those who have no knowledge or sensitivity to the revelation of God in his written word and in Christ Jesus. Hence, the Christian always has a moral contribution to make to the political debate over substantive justice, even though the contribution is in and of itself an imperfect appropriation of God's Word.

Second, one of the central themes of the Bible is that God calls his people to serve actively in the cause of building his kingdom of perfect righteousness. Thus, behind the conflicts and compromises of politics, there rests the metapolitics of God who in his providence is moving history toward the vindication of his righteousness. Insofar as Christians are called to be agents of the city of God within the cities of men, there is implicit therein the tacit assumption that God the Spirit can and will guide his servants to accomplish his ends. (Also, God used even his enemies to accomplish his purposes—something Christians all too often forget!)

Thus, the knowledge of our own moral inadequacy can never serve as an excuse for inaction based on moral agnosticism. God has spoken and has told us what he demands! However fragmentary our grasp of his truth, we are still called upon to act accordingly. But in so acting, we must at the same time act humbly with the knowledge that we always stand to be corrected. Hence, it is imperative that Christians respect the instrumental values of justice in the pursuit of substantive justice. For these very values protect us from the danger of moral arrogance seizing unwarranted power.

Accepting these self-imposed limitations, how then should Christians seek to bring God's standards of righteousness to bear on the political society? Should they seek to legislate morality? Can laws create a morally righteous society? Can the constraints of law backed by the force of the state be used to direct society to a fellowship of Christian love? For consideration of questions, we turn to the following chapter.

Chapter Four
Strategies
for Political Action

The previous chapters have sought to accomplish three basic goals. Chapter 1 reviewed the polarization which often occurs between theological liberals and theological conservatives over the question of how Christians and the church should relate Christian commitment to social and political problems. The chapter dealt with the weaknesses in both approaches as they are generally advocated, but insisted that political concerns are integral to the gospel. Chapter 2 identified some of the factors which have clouded the attempts of evangelical and conservative Christians when they have tried to work constructively in the areas of social and political ethics. Of particular concern here were the individualism, the negative attitude toward the state, pietism, and Gnosticism which are so often characteristic of conservative Christians. Chapter 3 dealt with the relationship between the nature of man and the nature of politics. It showed how conflict and compromise are inherent in the political processes of society's search for justice. And it identified procedural constraints which ought to characterize political activity when justice is being sought.

This chapter seeks to move beyond the theoretical to the practical. "Granted," one may say, "that the gospel relates integrally to the social and political plights of man. But how does one go about applying Christian concerns in the political world?" While chapters 2 and 3 may have seemed excessively abstract and theoretical to many readers, they provide necessary background for practical applications if one is to avoid the theological pitfalls which have been characteristic of so many past attempts at Christian political involvement. As the saying goes, "The road to hell is paved with good intentions!" Chapter 3, in particular, reminds us of the need for moral humility in our political endeavors. While Christians must speak and act forthrightly on social and political issues, they must at the same time guard against moral arrogance in presuming to speak the mind of God as it pertains to contemporary problems. While the previous chapters have focused generally on the *theological* underpinnings and justifications for social and political involvement, this chapter seeks to contribute to the *political* sophistication and understanding of such involvement.

Denominational Resolutions

One of the primary means the institutional church utilizes in relating the gospel to political issues today is that of mustering endorsements on behalf of certain policies and causes at church conventions and/or through denominational social-concerns boards. Once again, the liberal churchmen tend to praise such activity as a necessary part of the church's prophetic role in society. The conservative churchmen, on the other hand, tend to decry such efforts as inappropriate for a "spiritual" body. They insist that the church is not a political institution and that it should get on with its task of saving souls. The tensions between the two factions often lead to open confrontation in church councils, and sometimes even to church schism. Thus, in 1973, the Presbyterian Church in the United States (Southern Presbyterians) suffered a denominational split, one of the chief reasons rather clearly having been the social and political stands of the PCUS leaders. Citing the literature of the new "Continuing Church"—the conservative faction breaking from the PCUS—we read: "Today the Assembly [of the PCUS], through its boards, agencies and committees has replaced the Church's mandate to be first-of-all missionary and evangelistic, with a primary emphasis on social, economic and political mission." [1]

In chapter 1, we dealt with some of the theological justifications which both sides in such controversies offer for their positions on social and political engagements. We also tried to point out that missionary evangelism and political action can never be arbitrarily separated, as both sides to such controversy are often prone to do. But what is indeed ironic and tragic about such confrontations generated by the resolutions and pronouncements of denominations and church councils is that they are in effect little more than hot air! In terms of having any real effectiveness in the political world, such resolutions and pronouncements amount to little. Yet, in terms of damage done to the institutional church, they can be devastating.

There are at least six arguments which can be made against the practice of denominational and council pronouncements on social and political issues. *First,* the pronouncements themselves are generally not given the thorough and dispassionate consideration which is necessary if they are to make genuine contributions to the political debate of American society. Typically, a denominational social-concerns board writes drafts of resolutions for presentation at the annual church meeting. Too often, not enough is done to guarantee expertise in the initial draft of the resolution. Nor is there always a careful solicitation of viewpoints from different interests which might have light to cast on the pros and cons of the resolution.

Then the denominational social-concerns board reports the draft resolutions to the church convention. The leadership of the convention recognizes that the resolutions will likely cause intense debate, so the debate on the resolutions is usually scheduled for late afternoon on the closing day of the convention so as not to throw the program for other business off schedule. Only the most politicized of the delegates remain to debate the resolutions, and depending on what sort of majority controls the floor, ill-considered amendments and changes to the resolutions can occur with little or no thoughtful preparation. The next day, the press reports that the delegates of such and such a church have concluded that Angela Davis was the victim of political persecution, or that prayers in public schools should be restored. The truth of the matter is that any local county committee of a major political party probably brings as much if not more expertise to such an issue than an entire denominational gathering when it is governed under such sloppy and inadequate procedures.[2]

Second, denominational and council pronouncements often tend to be overly simplistic. One can predict that in the light of Watergate, church councils will condemn political fund-raising procedures used in this country and call for government-financed campaign spending. While there is obviously much merit to such a proposal, there are also difficulties and ambiguities. If we disallow private contributions to a political campaign, are we limiting the political freedoms of those who wish to contribute to a political campaign? Is funding to be channeled through the national committees of the major parties, or directly to individual candidates? The answer to this question would have a major impact as to whether or not we would foster party control or independent judgment of public officeholders. When one begins to recognize the complexities of most political issues, one next begins to ask where the church gets its vast moral prerogative to make official pronouncements on such issues.[3]

Third, denominational and council pronouncements are not necessarily representative of their constituency. In other words, in claiming to speak for all Baptists or all Methodists, one is, in fact, telling a lie. Just because conventions of other groups, such as labor unions or the American Medical Association, engage in the practice of making resolutions, it does not give the church license to do the same.

There are several reasons for the fact that "interest group" pronouncements often are contrary to rank-and-file beliefs and attitudes. First, all organizations suffer from what is called by social scientists "the iron law of oligarchy." The larger an organization gets, the more the business of the organization is delegated to administrative heads. Successors to the administrators are generally promoted from within the administrative bureaucracy. Before long, the "leadership" has lost touch with the rank and file. There is little the rank and file can do to recapture leadership inasmuch as the administrative and organizational machinery necessary for an effective challenge to the leadership is generally in the control of the leadership itself. To suggest that large denominational bodies are immune to this tendency is to be naive.

But within the typical Protestant denomination, there is another reason for the break between the rank and file and the leadership of the social-concerns committees. This gap occurs because the conservative "faction" of most denominations regards social and political pronouncements as inappropriate or pointless in the first place; so they do not seek appointment to such boards, leaving them completely in the control of the more socially and politically active liberal "faction." Thus, there is indeed some truth to the charge so often made by conservative churchmen that liberals have "taken over" the policy-pronouncement machinery of their denominations. However, they fail to recognize that this is not so much the result of a plot by the liberals as the result of the abandonment of potential influence by the conservatives.

Fourth, denominational and council pronouncements on social and political issues can be divisive and contrary to the well-being of the church, particularly when they are poorly handled. Thus, their potential for good must also be weighed against their potential for harming the well-being of the church. I have met several ministers who would never think of drinking a cocktail in front of their parishioners on the basis that some might take offense. In deference to their feelings, their behavior on this matter is usually quite discretionary. Yet when it comes to such matters as denominational pronouncements on controversial social issues, they feel little if any hesitancy in speaking out vigorously, insisting that the clergy must provide leadership on such issues for the church. Little regard is left for prudential restraint on behalf of protecting the unity and institutional well-being of the church. In fact, some clergy even view the institutional decline of the church in the wake of vigorous social pronouncements as a sign of health.

Fifth, denominational and council pronouncements on social and political issues are often used as rationalizations and excuses for the failure of the church to involve itself in more significant and meaningful forms of social and political engagement. Church leaders look to past resolutions and statements with pride as if their formal stands on issues provided some sort of moral absolution for more substantive failure in the obligation to minister to social and political needs. Since the churches have been unable to mobilize their constituencies for meaningful social and political involvement at the local and national level, they settle for words instead of deeds. Until denominational and council pronouncements can be brought into some meaningful relationship with the actual conduct of the Christian community, they are actually indictments of the church's own pious hypocrisy—and not the prophetic pronouncements on social injustice that their advocates insist.

Sixth, denominational and council pronouncements on social and political issues are generally ineffective at the political level. Community leaders and political decision-makers are not so naive as to be unaware that such resolutions are usually and generally ill-considered, simplistic, moralistic, and nonrepresentative of the grass-roots sentiment of the communities being represented. Such being the case, one can hardly expect resolutions to receive serious consideration. There are literally scores of denominational and religious lobby groups in the nation's capitol alone.[4] It is not unusual for them to take contrary stands on a number of issues (e.g., abortion, prayer in public schools, amnesty, busing, or Vietnam). A practicing politician looking for moral guidance cannot help but be cynical in such a situation when those claiming to speak with the voice of God are all busy saying different things. It is enough to make the most confirmed monotheist convert to polytheism! (Unless, of course, one defines God's omnipotence as including the ability to hold more than one opinion on the same subject matter at once.)

However, the preceding argument must not be interpreted as a simple indictment of any and all political activity on the part of the institutional church. There will no doubt be many evangelicals and conservatives reading this book who will agree with all of the preceding arguments and wish to let the case rest there. At least three provisos must be added at this point. *First,* it must be remembered that sociologically the institutional church is *ipso facto* a political institution in the sense that what it does has political significance whether it seeks such political influence or not. There can be no such thing as political neutrality in the church—for even when the church remains strictly silent on social issues, its very silence is a factor in the political climate of the nation. The withdrawal of the institutional church from politics has the same effect as the withdrawal of individual Christians from politics—it leaves the political world to institutions and individuals who do not share the moral concerns of Christian commitment. This in itself is a very important factor in the conduct of national politics.

Second, the preceding arguments against church resolutions and pronouncements as a means of social and political engagement must not be interpreted as a pat on the back for those evangelicals and conservatives who insist that the evangelizing mission of the church can be separated from social and political concerns. Chapter 1 argued that such concerns are integral to the gospel, and if the church is going to proclaim a full gospel, it must not neglect the social and political dimensions contained therein. Further, the very conservative churchmen who decry the social and political pronouncements of the "liberal" churches engage in similar activities of their own—although more subtly and covertly. The blending of right-wing politics with fundamentalist causes is a well-established fact of American church life, and the blending of "moderate" conservative political causes with "moderate" theological conservatism is also a well-established fact of American church life.[5]

Third, despite the procedural weaknesses and political ineffectiveness surrounding most denominational resolutions and pronouncements, there are some cogent arguments which can be made on their behalf. Resolutions and pronouncements can be used in attempts to stir the conscience of the Christian community to show what they *should* be doing as opposed to what they *are* doing. In this sense, they serve a prophetic function within the community. Further, they can serve as protestations of conscience from within the Christian community against the failure of the church to show true discipleship in the social and political spheres.

Understanding Christian Discipleship

But if we are going to find means of political and social involvement which are more honest and effective than simply passing church resolutions and pronouncements, we must begin by regaining a genuine sense of the full dimensions of Christian discipleship. We cannot talk merely about effective means of political action without first of all establishing true Christian motivations and concern for social and political questions.

We must rediscover the meaning of Christian discipleship. We must recognize that Christ called for a new divine order not only in our personal, inner selves but also in the entire spectrum of human affairs. We must recognize that the cross of Christ provides not only for our eternal salvation in the end but also establishes the pattern for our lives in the present. We must recognize that the bodily resurrection of Christ signals victory not only over death but also over all powers of evil. We must recognize that conversion cannot be separated from a discipleship which transforms one's *entire* life.

We begin this process through repentance of our past failures—not by pointing our fingers at those who have sinned in ways different than our own. And we must determine to reassess our political values and life-style in light of the complete counsel of God—not just the counsel of our own choosing.

In November, 1973, a number of evangelical leaders met to examine the failures of the church in political and social affairs and concluded that the immediate need of the Christian community was to develop a renewed consciousness of discipleship which recognized that the gospel addresses itself to the whole man. Accordingly, they issued a pastoral letter to their evangelical constituency calling for repentance, conversion, and renewed commitment to social justice:

A DECLARATION OF EVANGELICAL SOCIAL CONCERN[6]

"As evangelical Christians committed to the Lord Jesus Christ and the full authority of the Word of God, we affirm that God lays total claim upon the lives of his people. We cannot, therefore, separate our lives in Christ from the situation in which God has placed us in the United States and the world.

"We confess that we have not acknowledged the complete claims of God on our lives.

"We acknowledge that God requires love. But we have not demonstrated the love of God to those suffering social abuses.

"We acknowledge that God requires justice. But we have not proclaimed or demonstrated his justice to an unjust American society. Although the Lord calls us to defend the social and economic rights of the poor and the oppressed, we have mostly remained silent. We deplore the historic involvement of the church in America with racism and the conspicuous responsibility of the evangelical community for perpetuating the personal attitudes and institutional structures that have divided the body of Christ along color lines. Further, we have failed to condemn the exploitation of racism at home and abroad by our economic system.

"We affirm that God abounds in mercy and that he forgives all who repent and turn from their sins. So we call our fellow evangelical Christians to demonstrate repentance in a Christian discipleship that confronts the social and political injustice of our nation.

"We must attack the materialism of our culture and the maldistribution of the nation's wealth and services. We recognize that as a nation we play a crucial role in the imbalance and injustice of international trade and development. Before God and a billion hungry neighbors, we must rethink our values regarding our present standard of living and promote more just acquisition and distribution of the world's resources.

"We acknowledge our Christian responsibilities of citizenship. Therefore, we must challenge the mis-placed trust of the nation in economic and military might—a proud trust that promotes a national pathology of war and violence which victimizes our neighbors at home and abroad. We must resist the temptation to make the nation and its institutions objects of near-religious loyalty.

"We acknowledge that we have encouraged men to prideful domination and women to irresponsible passivity. So we call both men and women to mutual submission and active discipleship.

"We proclaim no new gospel, but the Gospel of our Lord Jesus Christ who, through the power of the Holy Spirit, frees people from sin so that they might praise God through works of righteousness.

"By this declaration, we endorse no political ideology or party, but call our nation's leaders and people to that righteousness which exalts a nation.

"We make this declaration in the biblical hope that Christ is coming to consummate the Kingdom and we accept his claim on our total discipleship till He comes."

The Church Congregation as a Political Unit

The beliefs and behavior of the Christian community must be awakened at the congregational level if we are genuinely going to reform the church. Resolutions and declarations may serve to prick the conscience of the church—but the really important thing is to transform the attitudes and conduct of Christian believers at the grass-roots level. If this is going to be done at all, it will have to be done where the "real majority" of Christians find the source of their spiritual fellowship and guidance—the local congregation.

Yet, we have too often separated our religious confessions and practices from real-life problems. We try, insofar as possible, to protect the church from politicization by refusing to consider serious social and political problems at all. The sociologist Jeffrey K. Hadden shows how this affects the quality of our preaching when he reports:

> While congregations seem to have little influence on a minister's political *beliefs*, the evidence is substantial that they affect his *behavior*. In spite of the fact that a large proportion of ministers feel that they should have the right to speak out on significant political issues, only a very small proportion actually do so. This discrepancy between belief and action apparently results from their desire to avoid head-on conflict with their congregations. It is as if an unwritten rule says that a minister is entitled to believe as he likes on political issues so long as he doesn't try to proselytize his own views.[7]

There are two things which are wrong with this situation. The first is that the congregation seems to have little opportunity to discuss political matters with the minister and thus influence his beliefs. The second is that the minister is not allowed to share his theological guidance in political matters with his congregation. In other words, the church has ceased to be a community in which Christians all serve to build one another up in the faith.

We must learn to face social and political issues directly at the congregational level. While the pulpit must never be allowed to degenerate into simply a political forum, it must nonetheless be supported as a place to speak courageously on social and political issues. While church schools and church discussion groups must never be allowed to degenerate into civic-affairs groups, they must nonetheless be encouraged to deal with difficult questions as to how Christian discipleship relates to the affairs of the community at large.

One may ask, "What difference does it make whether my denomination tells me via a resolution how to vote on an issue or my pastor tells me the same thing via the pulpit? Aren't they equivalent?" The answer is no. The minister speaking from the pulpit is speaking within the context of a community of discourse which allows open and honest dialogue to emerge on the issue under discussion. If he takes simplistic approaches to difficult and complex social problems, there is opportunity for exchange, interaction, and correction. Further, there is less likelihood that the minister will take extreme and simplistic solutions to problems if he is part of a congregation which has already made an honest attempt to develop a degree of political literacy, for his congregation will likely represent a blend of competing viewpoints and interests; and he will recognize that, if he is going to be even minimally effective, he will have to take into consideration the diverse opinions and convictions represented in the congregation.

Again, there will be those who object to this line of reasoning by stating: "If my minister is so restricted by competing viewpoints within the congregation as to be literally forced into Caspar Milquetoast social proclamations, what can be achieved by any discussion of issues?" The answer is really quite simple. *First,* one must recognize the tremendous amount of political illiteracy among the American populace at large. Only 53 percent of the eligible voters in the United States can even name their congressman. Less than 25 percent can tell how he voted on even *one* major piece of legislation in the previous year![8] When it comes to state and local matters, illiteracy runs even higher. Only as the American population becomes politically literate can it begin at all realistically to talk about reordering national priorities, solving the problems of racism, or making government more responsible to the people. Politics tends to become "special interest" politics because only those with special interests tend to be concerned with what the government is doing. Only those with more diffused interests can change this situation. The problem with American government is not that it is unresponsive, but that it has only special interests to which it responds. If the general public could be mobilized to stay attuned to political issues and developments, the policies pursued by the government would change accordingly. Thus, while discussion groups and the goal of raising political literacy do not sound very exciting, they are nonetheless very fundamental and basic ingredients to political reform.

Second, when such discussion takes place within the Christian community, there is the hope that Christian values and commitments will inform the direction and character of the discussion which takes place. While Christians will not always agree on all particulars when it comes to political goals and policies, they will nonetheless bring concerns to the political scene which might otherwise be un-represented and/or underrepresented in the political process.

Most people simply don't care about politics. One

of the reasons for this is that undoubtedly the political system seems to run well enough as it is without their involvement. Hence, a person may be tempted to make a simple trade-off between the time and effort it takes to be informed and involved and what he sees as the relatively modest and marginal gains he may make for himself and the community through his or her involvement. The Christian, however, dares not be so callous in weighing the balance. For if he is indeed called upon to make the concerns of his fellowman his own, he has a moral obligation to become involved in the political scene even if he sees no direct benefit to himself. The community leader and activist who gives of his time and energy sacrificially for the well-being of another is a twentieth-century good Samaritan! Until Christians in their local communities begin to understand and act on this basic notion, they should refrain from grandiose pronouncements on how to make this a better world.

How to Become Politically Active

It is one thing to become politically literate. It is quite another to become politically active. If the Christian community is to be true to the political imperatives of its faith, it must not be simply a hearer of the Word. It must be a doer of the Word as well. The usual failure of the church has been that it has sought political influence without giving opportunity for serious consideration of the facts and principles which underlie meaningful political involvement. The preceding section has emphasized the need for such consideration within the Christian community, particularly as it might take place within the local congregation. However, such efforts must not be a substitute for political action. Indeed, if practical modifications in the political behavior of the Christian community do not result from such efforts, then they are no improvement whatever over the flaunting of denominational and council resolutions.

Social scientists estimate that only about 1 percent of the adult population can be classified as political activists. Thus, in a community of 100,000 people (if we assume only 65 percent of the total population are adults), only about 650 individuals are actively following and participating directly in the political affairs of the community. In a community of one million people, only about 6,500 individuals would be properly classified as political activists.[9] Clearly, one congregation of Christians seriously committed to involving itself in community affairs can have influence beyond all proportion to its numbers!

But what means should Christians use to exercise their potential influence in the community? Christians should be cautioned, first of all, from the idea of entering the political world as a block engaged in some sort of holy crusade to usher in a new era in the political life of a community. We have emphasized repeatedly the proper educative role of the institutional church in focusing the attention of its members upon the social and political problems of the community. But when it comes to actually mobilizing for political action, there is reason to believe that the institutional church should show great restraint in becoming politically involved. The complexity of political questions and the conflict inherent in the political processes are such that while the church must encourage its membership to become knowledgeably involved in the political process, it should remain institutionally separate from particular political causes. This distinction is a fine line, of course. In extraordinary circumstances the rule will have to be violated, such as in the case of resisting political oppression or securing basic human rights. But even in these cases, it is important that the church as an institution associate itself not with specific political programs and parties per se, but with the principles of justice at the more abstract level.

The reasons for this are several. First of all, political problems are generally complex. The church as an institution does not have the resources or expertise, as a rule, to speak authoritatively to such problems. Second, because of the complexity of political problems, there is room for honest disagreement between men of goodwill as to how political problems will best be solved. The church gains nothing by arbitrarily choosing and advocating one solution over another. Its role is to continue to call society to the need for solving the problem, not to provide the solution itself.

These restraints would suggest, therefore, that while the church has an obligation to become involved at the educational and motivational level of politics, it has an equal obligation to separate itself from the implementational level of politics. Here the Christian lay person as a citizen of the world must act. He acts within the context of the shared insights of his fellow believers in the Christian community as stimulated by prophetic social proclamation from the pulpit. And he is upheld by the prayerful support of his congregation. The church, in turn, can measure its own success or failure to the degree that it produces men of Christian conscience who are willing to venture into the political world.

But how, then, can laymen become active in politics? One cannot give simple cut-and-dried answers to this question. The practice of politics is an art—not a science. And political strategies are the product of numerous factors depending on the political culture of each local community, the resources one has to work with, and the nature of the goals one is pursuing. It will be helpful, however, to discuss briefly the pros and cons of three basic routes to political involvement and action.

The Party Route. In the early years of the American republic, political parties were viewed with fear and trepidation by most of the nation's political leaders. Parties were seen as breeders of faction and pleaders for special interests. Upon leaving office after his second term as president, George Washington warned in his farewell address that parties should never be allowed to develop. In the nineteenth century, there was much less talk about doing away with political parties, but more by way of concern about how their "evil effects" could be regulated and controlled.

Parties were viewed as an unavoidable and necessary evil in a free society.

In the twentieth century, our attitude about political parties has changed considerably. We view open and competitive parties as a necessary characteristic of a liberal and democratic society. The "no party" and "one party" political systems suggest to the twentieth-century mind an authoritarian state which refuses to allow organized political dissent. Begrudgingly, we have come to acknowledge that political parties provide positive, necessary, and valuable services to a democratic society. Among other things, the parties provide organized "loyal opposition," help select and groom candidates for public office, mobilize the electorate at election time, and educate the citizens about the issues of significance. Clearly, when one considers the functions of political parties in our system of government, one of the means of influencing political decisions is by becoming influential in the political parties themselves.

But how does one achieve a position of influence within a political party? As strange as it may seem to the novice, entry to the party is very simple, and advancement in party ranks is very fluid. Political parties are usually like most churches—they'll welcome with open arms any warm body! Achieving a position of responsibility within the party is again usually just as simple as achieving a position of responsibility within the church—volunteer and you've got it!

Most party organizations in the United States

don't make formal requirements for membership—
no dues, no pledges for absolute party loyalty, no
ideological test. Instead, the parties generally
welcome anybody into their ranks who is willing to
call himself a "Republican" or a "Democrat." The
major parties in the United States are extremely
decentralized. One might even say that the national
parties are coalitions of the fifty state parties, and
that the state parties are coalitions of the county
organizations of which they are composed. The
parties are basically controlled from the bottom up—
not the top down. In terms of jurisdictional authority, American political parties are very similar to the
congregational concept of church order. The
denomination serves essentially as an "association"
of churches rather than as an arbiter of church policy
in such congregationally ordered churches. This
contrasts quite sharply with the episcopal form of
church order, for example, where the denominational authority serves as a form of church
discipline on member churches. In American
political parties, the national conventions are really
quadrennial gatherings of the local "congregational
units" of the party, in this case the state
organizations. The state organizations, in turn, are
really composed of delegates from the county
organizations.

One usually gets involved in party politics at the
local level by volunteering himself to the county
party. The county party organization is composed of
representatives from each of the geographic
precincts into which the county has been divided and

the candidates that party has placed on the ballot for partisan elections within the county. Since in most areas there are more precincts than volunteers to serve as precinct workers, one can usually secure some position within the party simply by volunteering. (Incidentally, it is just this factor which allows a few party leaders to control the local party organizations if they desire. Since there are usually more precinct positions open than volunteers, the party leaders appoint their personal friends to the vacancies. These friends, in turn, can be counted on to support the leaders at the annual county conventions.)

On paper, the duties of the precinct worker are quite elaborate. He is expected, among other things, to canvass his precinct to identify his party's supporters, to distribute party literature throughout the precinct at election time, and to encourage the party faithful in the precinct to vote on election day. In fact, however, this is not always done. Since the county organization plays an important role in nominating candidates for political office and getting them elected once they have been nominated, the precinct worker has an important voice in determining the quality of political leadership in his community. If he is not happy with the ticket, he is not going to be inclined to put himself out for the party. If he and other workers threaten to withhold support from the party if such and such a candidate is nominated for office, he can pressure the party into nominating and supporting candidates satisfactory to his criteria for community leadership.

The county organizations hold annual meetings at which time they select delegates to the annual state party conventions. The state party conventions nominate candidates for the state offices. In addition, every four years the state conventions select delegates to the national convention, which selects candidates for the office of president and vice-president of the nation.

Quite often one hears Christians who are un-initiated in party politics protesting that party involvement means selling one's soul to the party. We have all heard the remark, "I support the man, not the party" or "I vote the issues, not the party." While it is true that there are many party loyalists who can be defined as "party hacks," it is also true that there are many party activists who cannot be so classified. While the so-called "independents" often view themselves as above petty partisan politics and morally superior to those who are so involved, studies have shown conclusively that the indepen-dent as a rule is less knowledgeable about public affairs and less likely to become involved politically in any fashion whatever than the person who identifies with a party.

Involvement in party politics places the in-dividual into direct contact with many of the political leaders of his community. He can use these friendships as a means of influencing them on important political decisions. Further, since most local communities are under the domination of one political party, the real decisions on policies and candidates are often made within the party prior to the general elections. Because so few people recognize and take advantage of this fact, a very few Christians in a local party organization can have a significant influence on the moral climate of politics in their community.

The candidate route. An alternative to party politics, particularly at the local level, is that of becoming actively involved on an *ad hoc* basis on behalf of particular candidates for public office regardless of their party affiliation. School-board elections, for example, are usually nonpartisan. Sometimes, when a partisan primary election is very close, the party organization will remain neutral rather than risk the threat of splitting the party into factions. But more important is the fact that many office seekers who know firsthand how weak and unrepresentative the typical party organization tends to be are increasingly turning to personal campaign organizations in their quest for public office as opposed to depending on the party organization for their support.

In such cases, the political candidate must build his campaign organization from scratch. He needs people to canvass precincts, research issues, raise money, plan political advertising, and staff the campaign headquarters. A letter or a phone call to the candidate volunteering one's services, however modest they might be, will usually be acted upon immediately.

While working on behalf of an individual candidate does not give one the breadth of contacts that one achieves through normal party channels, it generally lends itself to a much more intimate relationship to the candidate himself than the diffused relationships of party involvement. The friendship and comradeship which develop between the candidate and his workers extend beyond the election when the workers can expect that their viewpoints and interests will receive active and serious consideration once the candidate reaches office.

The interest-group route. A third route to political influence is that of forming or becoming involved in an interest group. Virtually any organized group of individuals has the potential of becoming a political interest group—a local church congregation, the local Boy Scout den mothers, the Fraternal Order of Police, a pet club, etc. Political interest groups generally tend to concern themselves with one or two basic issue areas. Because of their specific interests, they can usually be much more forthright on behalf of particular interests than political parties which represent a much broader range of interests. Likewise, they can often be much more forthright than candidates or officeholders who have to deal with the conflicting demands of a broader constituency.

Interest groups seek to influence political decision making by any number of ways. They endorse parties or candidates which they believe to be sympathetic to their cause. Such endorsements are often followed up by financial contributions to campaign chests, use of mailing lists, and speaking engagements which candidates use for promotional purposes. Interest groups also give testimony at legislative hearings, initiate court actions, try to influence public opinions through letters to newspapers and magazines dramatizing their cause, and more.

The influence such groups command relates directly to the actual resources at their disposal—the amount of financial support they can offer, the size of the groups in terms of votes represented, and the ability to convince a candidate that the leadership accurately represents the feelings of the rank-and-file membership. This last mentioned resource is of particular significance, for most politicians can sense when the leadership of an interest group is speaking only for itself and not the rank-and-file membership. An example of this would be the labor-union movement. When the union leaders speak on bread-and-butter domestic issues, they are generally quite close to their constituency. But when they touch on matters such as civil rights or foreign policy, most politicians recognize that the leadership is speaking mainly for itself. Another example, already discussed above, is that of church denominational agencies speaking on behalf of their constituencies. Politicians recognize that the average lay member does not consciously follow the leadership of his church when making a determination as to how to vote.

By becoming active in groups such as the Americans for Democratic Action, the Americans for Constitutional Action, the Sierra Club, or Common

Cause, Christians can affect the actions and influence of such groups in the practical political world. Christians should also take seriously the possibility of forming their own interest groups which have as their goal the expressed purpose of bringing moral and ethical concerns to bear on political issues. Several such groups already exist. The Christian Government Movement (CGM) and the National Association for Christian Political Action (NACPA), for example, hold regular regional and national conferences bringing together officeholders and laymen to discuss particular political problems in the context of Christian understanding and commitment. The Christian Legal Society is an organization of Christian lawyers concerned with problems of legal reform. In the fifties and sixties, a group of Christian laymen in the Baltimore, Maryland, area formed the Christian Citizens of Baltimore, which concerned itself with recruiting able candidates for local political office and seeing that they addressed themselves to crucial issues of local concern. In the 1972 presidential campaign, several prominent ministers and laymen formed the Evangelicals for McGovern Committee on behalf of the Democratic nominee's candidacy. The use of interest groups having their origins from within the Christian community has been particularly noteworthy in the civil-rights struggle with the late Martin Luther King, Jr.'s, Southern Christian Leadership Conference and Jesse Jackson's Operation Breadbasket (now "PUSH") which grew out of it.

Once again, it should be emphasized how easy it is for an individual to become active either at the party, the candidate, or the interest-group level. The problem remains, however, that most people simply aren't concerned enough to become involved. One of the sorriest excuses which is often proffered is that of the church layman who says: "I give virtually my entire Sunday to the church. Wednesday nights I have prayer meeting and choir practice. And once a month, at least, I have a church social activity or board meeting. I just don't have time for community affairs."

The Christian community must learn to recognize that civic involvement is in itself a legitimate form of Christian service. To deny this is to suggest a truncated Christianity which arbitrarily separates the sacred from the secular. Such a viewpoint refuses to acknowledge that Christian calling and commitment pertain to all of one's life, not just what goes on inside the church walls. It makes the mistake, further, of placing the institutional interests of the church in competition with the needs of the community. It fails to recognize that the former is served only as it shares in the work of the latter.

The preceding discussion on practical political involvement has been very simple and elemental. But exactly at this point our involvement must begin if we are serious about bringing God's Word to bear on man's social existence. Moralists are all too often desirous of moving mountains without having to lift a finger. With indignation, they point to the decline of public morality and the crisis in American political institutions—but when it comes to doing something about them, they are seldom to be found.

The regeneration of American political institutions and an accompanying renewal of the American spirit will come about only when the American public begins to care enough to allow its vocalized concerns to transform themselves into political action. Just as faith without works is dead, so, too, moral indignation over evil without an accompanying struggle for the good results in nothing.

Politics is the organized struggle for the ascendancy of one's own self-interest over that of another. Justice, on the other hand, is the giving to every man his proper due. The Christian who enters politics must do so with the aim of achieving political justice. He does this by subjecting his own personal ambitions and desires to the scrutiny of God's revelation in the Scriptures. And as God gives the grace to do so, he learns to make the needs of his neighbor his own. In so doing, his search for justice becomes an act of sacrificial love.

Justice thus becomes the servant of love. Insofar as the Christian community commits itself to sacrificial love, it must also commit itself to the struggle for justice.

> "I hate, I despise your feasts,
> and I take no delight in your solemn assemblies.
> Even though you offer me your burnt offerings and
>   cereal offerings,
> I will not accept them,
> and the peace offerings of your fatted beasts
> I will not look upon.

Take away from me the noise of your songs;
to the melody of your harps I will not listen.
But let justice roll down like waters,
and righteousness like an everflowing stream."

Amos 5: 21-24, RSV

"You are the light of the world. A city set on a hill cannot be hid. Nor do men light a lamp and put it under a bushel, but on a stand, and it gives light to all in the house. Let your light so shine before men, that they may see your good works and give glory to your Father who is in heaven.

"Think not that I have come to abolish the law and the prophets; I have come not to abolish them but to fulfil them. For truly, I say to you, till heaven and earth pass away, not an iota, not a dot, will pass from the law until all is accomplished. Whoever then relaxes one of the least of these commandments and teaches men so, shall be called least in the kingdom of heaven; but he who does them and teaches them shall be called great in the kingdom of heaven. For I tell you, unless your righteousness exceeds that of the scribes and Pharisees, you will never enter the kingdom of heaven" (Matthew 5:14-20, RSV).

Notes

Chapter 1

[1] Woodrow Wilson as quoted in Clinton Rossiter, *Conservatism in America* (London: William Heinemann, Ltd., 1955), p. 244.
[2] Harris Poll as reported in *New York Post,* October 25, 1971, and *Gallup Opinion Index,* report no. 102 (December, 1973), p. 23.
[3] *Gallup Opinion Index,* report no. 70 (April, 1971).
[4] H. L. Nieburg, *Culture Storm* (New York: St. Martin's Press, Inc., Macmillan & Co., Ltd., 1973), pp. 1-2.
[5] Daniel P. Moynihan as quoted in "The Limits of Politics," *The Wall Street Journal,* June 20, 1969, p. 69.
[6] Henry A. Kissinger, "Central Issues of American Foreign Policy," in Kermit Gordon, ed., *Agenda for the Nation* (Washington, D.C.: The Brookings Institution, 1968), p. 614.
[7] Mark O. Hatfield, "Amnesty If . . . ," in Schardt, Rusher, and Hatfield, *Amnesty? The Unsettled Question of Vietnam* (Croton-on-Hudson, N.Y.: Sun River Press, 1973), p. 148.
[8] Samuel Lubell, *The Hidden Crisis in American Politics* (New York: W. W. Norton & Company, Inc., 1970), p. 296.
[9] Nieburg, *op. cit.,* p. 2.

Chapter 2

[1] See Louis Hartz, *The Liberal Tradition in America* (New York: Harcourt Brace Jovanovich, Inc., 1955).
[2] Billy Graham as quoted in David Lockard, *The Unheard Billy Graham* (Waco, Texas: Word, Inc., 1971), p. 97.

[3] Ferdinand Lassalle, *The Working Class Program* (1862), in Albert Fried and Ronald Sanders, eds., *Socialist Thought* (Chicago: Aldine-Atherton, Inc., 1964), p. 386.

[4] *New York Times*, May 20, 1916, p. 10.

[5] Richard B. Pierard, *The Unequal Yoke* (Philadelphia: J. B. Lippincott Company, 1970), p. 88.

[6] George W. Forell, *Christian Social Teachings* (Garden City, N.Y.: Doubleday & Company, Inc., 1966), p. 68.

[7] Billy Graham as quoted in Lockard, *op. cit.*, p. 124.

[8] Leighton Ford, *One Way to Change the World* (New York: Harper & Row, Publishers, 1970), pp. 34-35.

[9] *Ibid.*, pp. 51-52.

[10] *Ibid.*, p. 49.

Chapter 3

[1] The first significant call to renewed social concern on behalf of the evangelical community in the post-war period was Carl F. H. Henry's *The Uneasy Conscience of Modern Fundamentalism* (Grand Rapids, Mich.: Wm. B. Eerdmans Publishing Company, 1947). In the last five years, there has been a virtual renaissance of evangelical writing in this area, although it has lacked in dealing with the problems of how Christian conscience can be put into political action. Two of the more significant are David O. Moberg, *The Great Reversal* (Philadelphia: J. B. Lippincott Company, 1972) and Sherwood Wirt, *The Social Conscience of the Evangelical* (New York: Harper & Row, Publishers, 1968).

[2] On this, see Richard J. Mouw, "Evangelicals and Political Activism," *The Christian Century*, vol. 89, no. 47 (December 27, 1972), pp. 1316-1319.

[3] H. Emil Brunner, *Justice and the Social Order*, trans. Mary Hottinger (New York: Harper & Row, Publishers, 1945), p. 23.

[4] See Brendan F. Brown, ed., *The Natural Law Reader* (New York: Oceana Publications, Inc., 1960).

Chapter 4

[1] Quotations taken from the brochure entitled "Reaffirmations of 1973," published by the organizers of the "Continuing Church" advocates within the PCUS.

[2] On this general problem, see Paul Ramsey, *Who Speaks for the Church?* (Nashville: Abingdon Press, 1961).

[3] A respected political scientist, Reo Christenson, pleads for moral humility by church leaders in his article "The Church and Public Policy," *Christianity Today*, vol. 17, no. 7 (January 5, 1973), pp. 12-15.

[4] On this, see James L. Adams, *The Growing Church Lobby in Washington* (Grand Rapids, Mich.: Wm. B. Eerdmans Publishing Company, 1970).

[5] On this, see Jeffrey K. Hadden, *The Gathering Storm in the Churches* (Garden City, N.Y.: Doubleday & Company, Inc., 1969), chapter 3.

[6] This Declaration was adopted by roughly fifty evangelical leaders representing a broad spectrum of the evangelical community meeting in Chicago, Illinois, over the Thanksgiving weekend of 1973. Among the more prominent delegates signing this declaration were Frank Gaebelein, Carl F. H. Henry, Rufus Jones, Bernard Ramm, Paul Rees, Lewis Smedes, and Foy Valentine. This document may be quoted without permission.

[7] Hadden, *op. cit.*, pp. 89-90.

[8] *Gallup Opinion Index*, report no. 64 (October, 1970).

[9] Austin Ranney, *The Governing of Men*, Third Edition (New York: Holt, Rinehart and Winston, Inc., 1971), p. 294.